D0229876

LINCOLNSHIRE COUNTY COUNCIL
EDUCATION AND CULTURAL SERVICES.
This book should be returned on or before
the last date shown below.

SO2

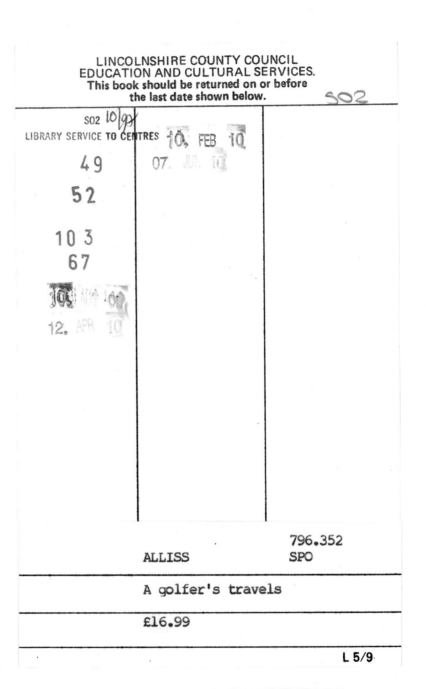

SO2 10/9?

LIBRARY SERVICE TO CENTRES   10, FEB 10

49   07. JUL 10

52

10 3

67

10   10

12. APR 10

ALLISS   796.352
                              SPO

A golfer's travels

£16.99

L 5/9

AD 02667054

A GOLFER'S TRAVELS
with
Peter Alliss

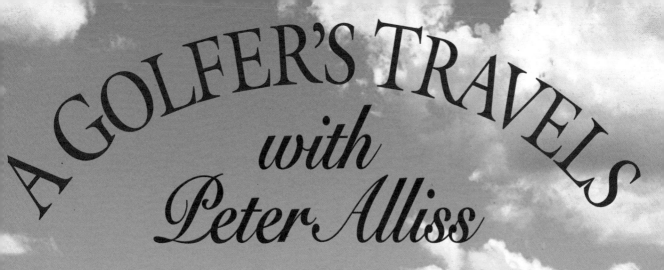

A GOLFER'S TRAVELS
with
Peter Alliss

PETER ALLISS AND JAMES MOSSOP

BOXTREE

LINCOLNSHIRE
COUNTY COUNCIL
796·352

First published in 1997 by Boxtree

an imprint of Macmillan Publishers Ltd
25 Eccleston Place, London SW1W 9NF
and Basingstoke

Associated companies throughout the world

ISBN 07522 1082 3

Text © Clearwater Images Ltd 1997

The right of Peter Alliss and James Mossop to be identified as Authors
of this Work has been asserted by them in accordance with the
Copyright, Designs and Patents Act 1988.

All rights reserved. No part of this publication may be reproduced, stored
in or introduced into a retrieval system, or transmitted, in any form, or by
any means (electronic, mechanical, photocopying, recording or otherwise)
without the prior written permission of the publisher. Any person who
does any unauthorized act in relation to this publication may be liable to
criminal prosecution and civil claims for damages.

1 3 5 7 9 10 8 6 4 2

A CIP catalogue entry for this book is available from the British Library.

Designed by Robert Updegraff
Printed and bound in Great Britain by Bath Press Glasgow.

Our thanks to the following photographers: Brian Morgan for
photographs in The Foreword and in Chapters 1, 2, 3 and 4; Phil
Sheldon for pictures in Chapter 5, Alexander Franklin for pictures in
Chapter 3, Scott D. Christopher for pictures in Chapter 2
(New Mexico) and Richard Maack for pictures in Chapter 2 (Arizona).

CONTENTS

Foreword

by Dr. Walter Hasselkus, Chief Executive, Rover Group.

It is a genuine delight to be associated with such an enthralling project as a book that gently steers many interesting people around some of the great golf courses in the world. That they are in the capable hands of Peter Alliss makes it even better.

7

As an international company our aim has always been to please our customers in 160 markets world-wide with a range of distinctive vehicles from Rover, MG and Land Rover, all of which demonstrate the best of British qualities that set them apart from other cars.

We feel very much the same way about the quality of this book and the TV Series and to see Peter behind the wheel in so many distant locations, often on unusual terrain, only adds to our pleasure.

When you have finished this great and wonderful escape to golf courses from North Britain to South Africa we hope that you, too, will agree that the car and the driver did a pretty good job of bringing a memorable golfing odyssey to life.

W. Hasselkus *(signature)*

DR. WALTER HASSELKUS.

Introduction

When the notion of travelling the world playing golf in exotic locations with famous people was first mentioned it seemed just a shade too fanciful to actually happen. Nip up to Skibo Castle in Northern Scotland and meet the Duke of York, jet across to Arizona where Gene Hackman has his clubs ready and, honestly, the '70s rocker Alice Cooper is waiting for you on the private, Hawaiian island of Lanai.

But it all happened and these few words are a preamble of our remarkable journey – written of course after we finally touched down at Heathrow at the end of a unique experience. Although I have done 'golf programmes' since 1974 (you may recall some of the 136 programmes through the years such as *Pro-Celebrity Golf* and *A Round With Alliss*) and TV commentary for even longer, this was the first time I had tackled such a venture, and these worldly wanderings were something else!

Within these pages, James Mossop and I are attempting to bring you the flavour of travel, adventure and excitement of the game of golf as well as introducing you to some unlikely places where the game is played. The enthusiasts of Rio Tinto (a golf course created on the site of a disused copper mine) for example, celebrating their first growth of grass – but only on the greens – was one of the typically unusual sights we saw.

Although I have been involved in golf since leaving school, it is amazing how many things still remain unseen, even for me. The golfing world may be small, but it embraces an astonishing mixture of countries and people from all types of backgrounds. Our senses were stimulated everywhere we went, from Scotland, Arizona, Spain, and Hawaii through to South Africa, with other pages on the Atlas marked down for future visits. I am sure, as with our experiences on recent journeys, there will be contrasts everywhere.

We will introduce you to our famous guests and others who are, perhaps, not as renowned, but just as keen on the game. We began with the entrancing Dame Kiri te Kanawa amid the raptures of Loch Lomond and ended the year in South Africa where our final guest was F.W. de Klerk, one of the overseers of the removal of apartheid and more than handy with his 7-wood. Elsewhere Alice Cooper, who has a handicap of five, told us of his reformed character and Admiral Alan Shepard re-lived the day he set foot on the moon, while the private and golfing lives of many others were revealed in the course of our interviews. There are people here who have made tremendous contributions to the game of golf as well as the changing face of the world we live in.

We experienced the delights of travel but even when you think you are on a magic carpet things can go wrong. Stranded for two nights in Mauritius, too bumpy to serve dinner over the Pacific Ocean, 5am alarm calls and 1am goodnights. At times such as this you realise that patience truly is a virtue.

We travelled a lot of miles, met a lot of people. We have turned over only a handful of willing stones and we realize there are many more things to do and see in this extraordinary world of golf. At least we have made a start. Enjoy.

PETER ALLISS

9

CELEBRITIES INVOLVED
HRH Duke of York
Dame Kiri te Kanawa (opera singer)
The Very Rev. James Simpson (Moderator of the Church of Scotland)
Dan Quayle (former vice-president of the United States)
Lyle Anderson (owner of Desert Mountain and Loch Lomond)
Admiral Alan Shepard (retired astronaut)
Gene Hackman (actor)
Steve Redgrave (Olympic oarsman)
Jaime Ortiz-Patino (owner of Valderrama)
Alexsandr Pavlovich Vladislavlev (Russian diplomat)
Martin Pareja Obregon (matador)
Alice Cooper (rock star)
Hootie and the Blowfish (rock band)
Benjamin Cayetano (Governor of Hawaii)
Sir Garfield Sobers (cricketer)
Gary Player (golfer)
F.W. De Klerk (leader of the opposition in South Africa)
Andrew Mlangeni (Member of Parliament in South Africa).

THE PRINCE AND THE DAME

HRH The Duke of York recalls with anecdotal warmth a moment early in his golfing career. He was chipping away on a patch of grass at Windsor Castle when his father, HRH The Duke of Edinburgh, called out to him as he drove past with his carriage horses, 'I've got some golf clubs for you.' The young Duke was puzzled and felt compelled to ask where they might be stored: 'I said that's very kind but where do you keep them? I was expecting a set of the late King's hickory shafts but in fact he meant that he was passing on the patronage of several of the Royal courses.'

We were in the library at Skibo Castle in the far north of Scotland, close by Dornoch Firth and just a few miles from the historic Royal Dornoch Golf Club where in June you can play golf until almost midnight. Our day was one of eerie mists and slanting rain, which seem to be a summer speciality in Sutherland.

The Duke of York revelled in the fun of a three-ball partnership with myself and the Very Reverend Dr James Simpson, Moderator of the Church of Scotland and a tidy golfer with a professorial knowledge of Royal Dornoch where he has played with the Duke in the past.

The journey to the mainland's most northerly golf course at Durness, to Skibo and Dornoch, revealed the natural beauty of the area with the elegance of the castle and the sheer joy of the golf course. The Duke, who had driven up from the Royal Family's summer holiday at Balmoral, was not accompanied by the tabloid *paparazzi* who tend to dog his every movement.

Royal Dornoch: mist and rain a speciality, but an outstanding golf course.

Perhaps we should check the loft of this Royal lethal weapon.

At Dornoch there was complete freedom. A few members and locals stood in the mists as the Duke fiddled with his grip on the first tee. He is a strong hitter and, with the opening hole of 331 yards into the wind and damp, he needed to be. He hit his opening tee shot an impressive 210 yards, leaving himself an 8-iron of 92 yards to the front of the green. On a calm day a simple wedge would have been the club. He putted five feet past, missing the hole on the left, and stood looking fairly disgusted with himself, as you might expect from someone who has an official handicap of 7.4 at Royal Liverpool. Against all previously known putting form I managed a birdie three and the good Dr Simpson will not thank me for recording his double bogey six after he failed to get out of a bunker.

As the Duke walked on to the second tee for a shot of 167 yards to the par-three hole he admitted: 'I'm a bit vulnerable on these.' He still managed a par and all those lessons he had been taking from the Silvermere professional, Doug McClelland, were clearly visible from the studied way in which he was playing.

Alas, I encouraged those thoughts too soon. Off the tee of the third hole he hooked his drive into gorse that was still struggling to recover from a spell in winter when winds straight from Red Square had dropped the temperature to 20° Fahrenheit below freezing. It was a quick snap-hook, the private torture of the powerful hitter and he said straight away: 'Oh, no. Reload. I've got a mental aberration with this driver. That ball isn't even worth looking for.'

By now the clubhouse was enveloped in mist and although his ball was lost, his sense of humour hadn't gone with it. The Duke spotted our cameraman, Chris Topliss, and his sound engineer, Keith Conlon, linked to each other by the cable that ran between their equipment and announced that it would be fun to 'sever the umbilical cord to see you two fall all over the place'.

The rain got heavier. There was a distant rumble of thunder and the Duke called everyone together to suggest that if it came any closer we would walk in. He took off his Navy sweater and put on his Ryder Cup rainsuit. After six holes we cut across to play the 13th and 14th before submitting to the elements. When the Duke invited two women golfers, playing their monthly medal, to go through ahead of us I was not sure that they recognized him. They did, though, when they came into the clubhouse and saw us all having tea and shortbread.

I was impressed with his enthusiasm for the game and I hope he will not be offended if I liken him to Sean Connery in saying that the handicap flatters the skill. He would be a very dangerous player off 10 or 12 because he is capable of getting a few birdies. He has a genuine passion for the game, which came through comprehensively when we talked at Skibo.

13

A flowing follow through shows the single-figure Duke of York at his best.

In the library back at the castle, the Duke proudly wearing his Royal and Ancient Golf Club tie, I asked him about his involvement with golf, how it all started and what sense of reward he got from the game. I have always been impressed with his manner and his desire to become a golfer proficient enough, perhaps, to qualify for the Open Golf Championship. I liken him to a playful Irish setter. He has handsome looks, he is fit but just occasionally appears a little immature.

He began: 'My grandfather was a particularly good golfer and my uncle was a good golfer. There's been a bit of a gap and I took it up quite by accident. We have a golf course at Windsor and another at Balmoral on which the Household play. When I was a child I would go round occasionally with one or two clubs but the game never really caught my imagination. I had a 5-iron and a borrowed putter before I had my first set of clubs, which was only a few years ago. It happened through my observer-navigator-tactician when I was with HMS *Campbeltown*. We were forming the flight and team building and he told me he played golf and used to play off two as a county junior. Since joining the Navy, he said he had gone up to six. We went off to hit a few balls one day and he could see that I was completely hooked, not dissimilar to a salmon, from day one. That was six years ago.

'I suppose I mucked around and played at home at Windsor and Balmoral during 1989 and 1990. But the first time I took my game into the public domain, as it were, was when HMS *Campbeltown* visited Liverpool in 1990 for the Battle of the Atlantic weekend. I played on a private course in Cheshire and then went to Hoylake [Royal Liverpool] the next day. I have to say that it is a somewhat difficult course to start on. But everybody at the club was incredibly friendly and it was a pleasure to go there and play for the first time. On the opening hole you play immediately across the front of the clubhouse which would be daunting for most people but was even more daunting for me. There were lots of people standing in the main clubhouse and on the putting green watching. My ball landed directly outside the members' window, still on the fairway, I might add. To a man and woman they all went back into the clubhouse and maintained a respectful distance so that I was not embarrassed by a huge crowd for my second. It was a daunting process.'

I had to ask whether in his attempts to control the little white ball, he had managed to control himself. You know, no club throwing or swearing

tantrums that the frustration of it all tends to induce. He said: 'I went through about six months of – well, I'm extremely hard on myself. My wonderful coach, Doug McClelland, is forever saying to me, "Look, it's not a rifle that you have in your hand." I'm a bit of a perfectionist and always wanted the ball to land where I intended it. I went through a frustrating period of not being able to work out what I was doing wrong. I've got a little more experience now and I'm beginning to understand about the control. I went through a period of getting cross. If I throw a golf club I walk off the course there and then on the grounds that I think I have behaved extremely badly and it's not a thing that somebody should do. I've thrown a golf club once and I felt so ashamed. I've occasionally taken the head off a daisy but I don't think that's throwing a club.

'Standing on the practice ground at times, particularly at the end of a long week at work, is quite a good way of relieving stress and it doesn't make any difference where the ball goes at that stage. I'm just interested

The library at Skibo Castle with the Duke praising his tutor, Doug McClelland.

in working out the frustration and then I'll concentrate and perhaps have fifteen to twenty minutes of good golf at the end. Then I'm quite happy.'

A game that suits his personality, perhaps? I remember Dan Maskell, the tennis commentator, remarking that HRH Princess Royal might well have been able to reach the Wimbledon semi-finals if she had stayed with the game instead of concentrating on equestrianism.

'I must say that if you look at various people's personalities and games, as it were, to fit them, I suppose I'm more of an individual than a team player. I wasn't particularly good at team sports when I was at school. I didn't play football very well. I was a reasonable cricketer but, again, that's very much an individual game within a team. I have to say that even I had lessons from Dan Maskell at Wimbledon – and I've played on the Centre Court at Wimbledon – but I don't remember being very good at it. I think Anne was very good. She is good at that sort of thing and she can apply herself and she made it as a rider in no uncertain terms.

'I used to ride, but as a young boy I suffered from hay fever and if I came off in long grass I was dead for a day. It left me rather than me leaving it, because every time I got near a horse I sneezed. It was just easier to avoid sneezing.

'My father was quite surprised when he saw me practising golf at Windsor Castle. As a result I now have a bucket of earth and grass seeds so that I can replace any divot I might make. He likes to practise his driving and his dressage on the same ground so there is a sort of queue to see who can use the practice ground. He used to take cover every now and again when I first started because he would be driving up the road and the ball didn't always go in the right direction. He was good encouragement, I think.

'I'd love to go and play all the courses. The first club I was made patron of was Royal Liverpool and I keep my handicap there, or try to. The secretary is always doing nasty things to it based on other people's information!'

Could he put the whole package together? The bunker shot, reading a green, visualizing a shot? 'Yes,' he said, without hesitation. 'Doug McClelland said very early on, that the only way to improve your golf is to go and play on the golf course and not on the practice ground. If you can take what you do there on to the course, that's quite good. I've got to the stage where I can actually get from the tee to the fairway or the light rough and I can then get to within striking distance of the green with my second shot, or my third if it's a par five. Where I need to concentrate now is close to the green. That's where my handicap is going to come down. When you work out that almost half of the game is putting, how much time does one spend on practising putting? Not very much because people are more interested in driving the ball or hitting irons on the range. I'm concentrating on the short game, the chipping the putting, the pitching and trying to get down in two from around the green. I give myself tests now.'

We went on to discuss the golf courses at Windsor, of which Mint Ferguson was the architect, and Balmoral.

The Duke told me, 'I discovered recently, that the first record we have of a golf course at Windsor Castle was in 1901. The course was laid out differently then, but at the beginning of her reign, the Queen put in some paddocks for horses and the course was slightly altered to accommodate them. There is no par five but there are holes of 400 yards and you can hit your driver. Balmoral is mostly grass. There's no heather but quite a lot of trees. In an effort to split the sixth and seventh fairways, the Duke of Edinburgh planted a copse of trees. When the then Prime Minister, Harold Wilson, played golf shortly after it was planted, he named it "Philip's Folly" because his ball would always end up there.

17

'At the moment I'm in the fortunate position of being asked to play in all sorts of places so as yet I don't have a favourite course, but I play most at Swinley Forest, which is just behind Ascot. It's quiet. There aren't many people to disturb one and one can always get away from the hubbub of life. You can switch off with golf because golfers are not interested in who you are. They're more interested in how you play the game. That's wonderful. It's like being in the Navy to a certain extent in that you cannot do your job in the Navy unless you are professionally able. There is no way I could ride on the laurels of just being the Duke of York. My observer Wayne Sheridan, who has now left the Navy, and I still have an annual match and if you want to know about gamesmanship you should look at that one. It starts two or three days if not months before, about who is going to win. I actually sorted him out this year, 5 and 4, not quite a dog licence [7 and 6] but I was quite pleased with that!'

His mention of the Navy prompted me to ask the Duke how he felt at the prospect of retirement, and how he thought his experience in the Falklands might have affected him.

'Life is a learning process,' he replied. 'It doesn't matter how old you are you learn something every day. Much the same as a sharp rock comes off the side of a mountain, it tumbles downwards, its edges are chipped off and after a time in the sea it becomes rounded and smooth. The Navy has done a lot of chipping and hacking at my sharper edges. Anybody who gets an opportunity to join one of the services would find me recommending it, purely because it teaches you a lot about yourself – and there's nothing like going to war to learn about yourself. By 1999, I'll have done twenty years. It's quite a long time but it's a career. That's what careers are supposed to be.

Is there anything he would particularly like to achieve on the golf course?

'I'll never win the Masters because I don't think I'll be a professional or a good enough amateur. But if I have the inclination, the time, the ability, enough play and practice, I would like to qualify for the Open Championship. It doesn't matter what stage – just one.

A word of advice from the Very Rev. James Simpson, Moderator of the Church of Scotland.

'I've always had to play off the first tee with a crowd. Somebody's always interested in the fact that I'm going to play the game. The golfing media are excellent because they understand when to be quiet and when to take their photographs but the normal media hacks who follow us around, the photographers, don't know so you get this cacophony of sound before you've hit a shot. I've learned to put up with it. It's very good exercise, trying to put them out of your mind.'

At this point, we embarked on a technical discussion. The Duke has a driver with a 10.5 degree loft, but says the shaft is too whippy and he confessed that much of the modern jargon, torque rating and so on, is

The practice ground is a good place for working off the week's stress, says the Duke.

beyond him. He went on to tell me about his first meeting with Doug McClelland:

'When I first started to play and mucked about, my police officer said to me: "Look, if you're going to play this game you're going to do it properly and you're going to get lessons." I told him I didn't need lessons. You just hit the ball and all that. Anyway, I said, "Who in the world is going to come here and give me lessons?" He told me his father-in-law was the weekend starter at Silvermere, a public course in Surrey, and knew the professional, Doug McClelland. The call was made and the first lesson arranged for two thirty on Sunday afternoon, with Doug to present himself at Shaw Farm Gate. I've since heard Doug's version of this conversation. Now he's nobody's fool and when he had a request to appear at Shaw Farm Gate, Windsor Castle, to give the Duke of York a golf lesson he sensed an element of leg-pulling. He suggested to his wife that they take an afternoon drive, calling in at the gate just in case it wasn't a hoax. He walked across to the gate-keeper and said, "I've had this request to come and give the Duke of York a golf lesson but I have a feeling . . ." '

Doug, the Duke said, had been informed that it was true and was asked if he would mind following the police officer through Home Park to the castle where the Duke was waiting. Doug may have been surprised at this turn but not as surprised as he was fifteen minutes into the lesson when HM the Queen came round the corner with her dogs. The Duke and Doug have been student and teacher ever since, although the Duke occasionally takes advice from Bernard Gallacher, the former Ryder Cup captain and, until recently, head professional at Wentworth. They played together recently and Gallacher quickly spotted that the Duke had become flat with his driver.

Are Princesses Beatrice and Eugenie swinging golf clubs yet?

'A few years ago I played a game of golf and afterwards a man sitting not far from me handed me a small set of clubs for Beatrice. I said, "Thank you very much, Mr. Alliss." Since then I've been cursing Mr Alliss because I now have two daughters. Shortly after you gave the clubs to me I had to ban the girls from using them because Prince William was struck on the head with a putter – but I thought they were too dangerous anyway: I could see them swinging round and clouting each other on the head. Since then, if I want to go and practise, Beatrice

wants to go out and hit a few balls as well. While I've been at Balmoral, chipping and putting, they've both been out and I've been giving them the odd tip and lesson. They can hit it. They can get the ball off the ground. There's a good deal of healthy competition. I was down at the far end of the cricket field hitting a few 7-iron and 8-iron shots and had just given Eugenie a quick tip when Beatrice appeared. A furious row developed about who was the better player. I have now to get them each a new set of clubs so that they can start together. The competition is ghastly. I've vowed never to teach them to drive. I'll ask their grandmother and grandfather to do that. I'll teach them to play golf, sort of. They enjoy it and they're both very good for their ages. I'm not going to push it because it's not something I want to force down their throats. If they want to play then I'm more than happy to give them the odd tip. They've got the patience and the application, even at their ages, to play a nice little round.'

'The Queen Mother did something quite remarkable in the summer of 1996. She was talking to Colonel Johnston one day after church, discussing Swinley Forest with him where he was due to play. "Oh," I heard her say, "do they still have that splendid cold buffet they had when I played there in 1920?" Sir John suggested she went back with him to find out. They duly returned after I had been canvassed about the content of the 1920 version. She had a lovely lunch but I'm not sure it was an exact replica of seventy-six years earlier.

'The Queen Mother is a wonderful story-teller. I love her dearly. She has such a wealth of experience to share, even with Beatrice and Eugenie. What she has and says belongs to folklore and should be left that way rather than taped for posterity. I'm a great believer in that there are certain

As I was saying, or was I listening?

21

The grandeur of
Skibo Castle.

things that should be recorded and others that should not. That's life. The game of golf is the game of life. Life is unfair. Golf is unfair.'

The Duke of York is always good-natured, even when probed about his future. He said, 'There may be more for me in the Navy, I don't know. I've thought about all sorts of different things but quite a lot of the avenues that one would look at often get closed off for practical reasons rather than philosophical ones. And one is always looking for good ideas. The leisure business is one and I haven't looked at it particularly closely. I have a reasonable ability at golf and therefore if I was going to do something with sport or the leisure, if you want to use that term, then golf would be what I would most likely go into. But it would be quite judicious as to where and what and how. It is very difficult to pinpoint at the moment.

Finally, was there anything about golf that he *didn't* enjoy? 'Slow play. I have a very close liaison with the R and A, of which I'm an honorary member and I'm in fairly frequent conversation just to keep up with the bugbears of golf so that if I'm going to a dinner I can make one or two points for them. One of the things that comes up most is slow play. People shouldn't necessarily rush round golf courses but there should be a flow to the game rather than standing behind every shot and trying to copy what you see on television. I had one experience of slow play at Swinley Forest where I started at the ninth. A society was visiting and I was playing with Bernard Gallacher so we drove out to the ninth. We were held up over 15, 16, 17 and 18. On the 18th, for some strange reason, they invited us through. As they were at the end of their round it seemed a belated gesture. We played up and finished the hole, and as Bernard was walking towards the next tee and I was leaving the green, one of those who had allowed us through asked me: "Is that Bernard Gallacher over there?" I told him it was, and he thanked me. As I walked away I heard him say, "Hey, guys, that's Bernard Gallacher over there," to which a member who'd been near the green, watching, said, "Yes, and that's the Duke of York you've just asked."

'There are amusements, you see, but it's wrong if people are playing slowly and know they are. I'm always conscious of who's coming up behind in case they want to play through. There's an awful lot to learn around the game of golf and it takes time to know about etiquette, slow play and so on. It needs to be taught to the younger player straight away. Slow play is always a problem and it's not just a matter of encouraging people to keep the flow going.'

Soon the Duke of York had to leave Skibo Castle and Royal Dornoch to go back to Balmoral and his daughters. We had appreciated his forthrightness and gentle humour.

The flag above Skibo Castle, and at the Carnegie golf club, is British on one side, American on the other, which gives an indication of the number of transatlantic visitors and members. Andrew Carnegie, a Scot, had lived in America for some time when he came home in the spring of 1897 to discover Skibo Castle just forty-five minutes north of Inverness. He described the place as 'Heaven on Earth', bought it for just £85,000, and gave his name to the golf club.

The castle is now owned by Peter de Savary, who has tried to maintain many of the old traditions of hospitality, comfort and warmth. A guest is no sooner through the front door than a pleasant young Scottish butler is suggesting a drink. Dinner is preceded by a toast to Andrew Carnegie.

The 7000 acres of the estate, including the golf course, teem with fascinating flora and fauna. Among the 130 species of lichen, some are extremely rare. In November an estimated 16,000 widgeon from Iceland congregate on the Firth. There are greylag geese and, on shore, roe deer, otters, pine marten and foxes are seen. But if that is enough to take the golfer's mind away from his game, the challenge of the Carnegie links will soon bring back the sense of purpose every golfer feels when they sight the first tee – in this case a par four of 449 yards, usually deceptively downwind. The championship tees give the course a length of 6671 yards and a par of 72. The views are a stunning plus, perhaps specially so on the narrow, winding road to Durness, where sheep may stray and there are passing places every 100 yards or so. Durness, not far from Cape Wrath, is a nine-holer with 18 tees, 100 members at £60 a year and green fees of £10. There is no bar, and no telephone, but an abundance of fun. The members – villagers, crofters and fishermen built the clubhouse themselves for £45,000, and pursue their pars and birdies with a passion the Duke of York would fully understand and appreciate.

OVERLEAF The 18th hole at The Carnegie Club could be a postcard setting.

25

Dame Kiri te Kanawa loved every moment of her sail across Loch Lomond.

A soft, Scottish morning was two-stepping between absolute July and contrary April, and the small boat came tootling round one of the loch's little peninsulas before gliding to the wooden jetty as stately as the family of swans that made way for it. An explosion of sunlight enhanced the scene as the clouds separated and I waited for Dame Kiri Te Kanawa to step ashore. It was a joy to pick up again on our twenty-year friendship. The backdrop was theatre itself. Loch Lomond's deep and mysterious waters shimmered in the light, while the old mountain to the North, Ben Lomond, seemed to gaze down in presidential approval as we made our way along the gravel path to Rossdhu, the house built in 1773 as the family home of the chiefs of the Clan Colquhoun and now the clubhouse of a golf course. Take the majesty of the setting, the creative design of the golf course and the history of the house, and you may wallow in some kind of paradise, a secluded world just thirty-five minutes from Glasgow Airport.

We enjoyed to the full, even driving to the opposite side of the loch and the tiny village of Balmaha to help George, the postman, deliver the afternoon mail on his red-funnelled boat, *Marion*, that looked as if it had been plucked from the pages of a children's story book.

Rossdhu has myth and legend in its foundations. It stands by the ruins of the old castle and looks out to islands where anyone strolling on the shoreline today might believe that peace had prevailed for ever. Then they tell you of the tragedy and pain of the Colquhouns. It was on Inchmurrin that the tenth chief, John Colquhoun, was murdered by a band of marauding Hebrideans led by the Macleans as he tried to negotiate a peace. And, during Queen Victoria's time, Sir James Colquhoun was drowned with four of his gillies while returning from stalking deer on Inchlonaig.

The treasures of years – ornaments, tapestries, paintings, furniture and trinkets – decorate the house and Dame Kiri, in golfer's attire of bottle-green plus twos and sweater, sank into her drawing-room chair to drink it all in.

However, outside had become more July than April, and the golf course, designed by the Americans Tom Weiskopf and Jay Morrish, was beckoning. It has been described as the best inland course in Britain and few would argue with that. An American magazine has nominated it as number one of the top ten selected courses developed since 1992. It is parkland with knobs on.

Weiskopf won the Open Championship at Troon in 1973 and had been a Ryder Cup player. He stayed on the site for three months and when the 7060 yards of golfing real estate was completed, he said: 'I consider Loch Lomond to be my lasting memorial to golf. My aim, as the first American to design a course in the very home of golf was to make it a thinker's course. It demands strategic play and calls for every club in the bag to be used as the course works its way through some of the finest property I have ever laid eyes on with some of the oldest and most majestic trees in Scotland.'

There is certainly much more than scenery to Loch Lomond. The par five 6th hole, which runs along the banks of the loch, is at 625 yards, the longest hole in Scotland; a genuine three-shotter. Weiskopf and Morrish have balanced that with two par fours, the 9th (340 yards) and the 14th (345 yards) that are driveable by the bravehearts.

The designers were so impressed with the challenges offered by the 14th that they called it 'Tom and Jay's Choice'. By the way, it is here that Weiskopf almost lost his life when he sank deeply into the marsh. Today, the player is given the option of risking a big hit directly across the marsh or taking the cautious route to the left, with a delicate chip required, to a narrow green. To the professionals it could be anything from an eagle two to a double bogey six and more. No further testimony is needed although Sandy Lyle, a winner of majors on both sides of the Atlantic and a Scot who might have been born with a club in his hand, simply underlined the creators' faith when he said: 'If I had to play the same course every day of the year I would not have to look much further than Loch Lomond. Not only is the setting magnificent but the quality of the design and the maintenance of the course makes it a pleasure to play. It is truly a fair test of golf for both amateur and professional alike.'

As we set out with our clutch of Loch Lomond caddies, Dame Kiri and I could see the clarity of Sandy's appraisal all around us. The design is so

OVERLEAF The picturesque 10th at Loch Lomond; Arn Burn it is called.

29

imaginative, with its choice of tees, that for the inaugural Loch Lomond World Invitational in September 1996, won by the Dane Thomas Bjorn, it was a par 71. From the front tees, however, the yardage becomes 5595 yards with a par 74 for women.

Using the wisdom of years, I decided to play from the medal tees (6730, par 72) and Dame Kiri moved forward, admitting that she had not had a game for a year and that the 12-handicap to which she previously played had developed considerable rust. Still there was a delightful feel about the place and I seemed to have the right touch with my irons, so much so that one of the caddies wondered why I was not out there collecting cheques on the European Seniors tour. That brought a smile or two. Dame Kiri wanted to set the scenery to music, especially as we wandered along the 10th fairway and waited for the green to clear: 'It is so natural. If this was Switzerland there would be cowbells and things but this is just perfect. You look at Augusta National and you think you could package it up and place it anywhere but this is wild. You cannot manufacture this.'

I liked her swing and it quickly became clear that with a couple of minor adjustments, she would be a very good golfer. She told me that, over the next few years, she intends to work at the game. It must be perfect relaxation for someone with such a heavy and demanding international schedule. However, the time did not seem quite right to point out that her left hand was a touch too far under the shaft at address. I've always found that if you try to change people during a round it can throw them completely. But Dame Kiri promised herself to practise a bit more and become more consistent. She was going to take lessons which was something she'd been telling herself to do for the last five years.

The 10th hole at Loch Lomond is called Arn Burn, after the stream that widens to a pond on the left of the fairway. There are attractive stone bridges, finches flit among the trees and all around is the sound of silence. It is a par four of 405 yards for the men and 385 yards for the women. We played it well. I joked with Dame Kiri about my 'power fade' to a perfect fairway position and told her that she couldn't fail if she took the club back nice and slowly, paused at the top and swept through it. The drive was neat and straight, not very high but far enough for her to take her 5-wood for the second shot, which left her a chip and two putts for a five (nett four) to halve the hole. When I hit my 5-iron approach 170 yards pin high,

I thought I might have nipped her with a birdie. Still, the shot was good enough for me to consider going on a diet. It was one of a series of delightful holes with evocative names such as Yon Bonnie Banks, which is the seventh running alongside the loch and Gallows Hill, a par five with 14 bunkers, whose name says everything.

We paused for a picnic lunch of salad and fine wine, next to the Bay, a par three with a long carry over marsh to a well-bunkered green alongside an attractive inlet. At 205 yards from the championship tee, it is clearly not for the faint-hearted.

Finally, we decided that the match had ended in a friendly all-square and it was time to help George deliver the mail. On board the little mailboat there was plenty of time to appreciate the largest and one of the loveliest lochs in Scotland. The hills that slope away to the south are gentle and rolling. To the north and east, the hills rise with a special wooded drama all of their own. There are thirty islands, and at places between them the water is 630 feet deep. There are attractive bays and the waters are said to be heavily populated with trout, pike and powan, a white fish found in Scottish lochs and Welsh lakes.

A pause, as Dame Kiri admires the scenery from a groundsman's cart.

It is said that the song 'Loch Lomond' was composed by one of Bonnie Prince Charlie's followers on the eve of his execution in Carlisle gaol. The 'low road' is supposed to be the path by which his spirit would return to his native Scotland after his death, much quicker than the 'high road' taken by his friend.

Our voyage on the mail boat, in the afternoon with a modest breeze, was restful, a time to talk as *Marion* chugged away from the land past moored dinghies and skiffs and into open water. Dame Kiri is a wonderful companion. She is jolly and her easy-going naturalness seems remarkable when you consider how far her career has taken her since she started out from the New Zealand town of Gisborne. She has made countless recordings and has sung major roles at the Royal Opera House, Covent Garden, the Metropolitan Opera, New York, the Paris Opera, San Francisco Opera, Sydney Opera, Cologne Opera and La Scala in Milan.

We chatted about opera, family and life in general. When you think of a female opera star the image of a large, temperamental prima donna usually springs to mind. But Dame Kiri, whose 'Now is the Hour' at the end of the 1990 Commonwealth Games made hard men cry, is the complete opposite, one of the most understated world-famous performers you could ever hope to meet.

She is fun and gentle, loves life and nature: an isn't-it-good-to-be-alive person. I sometimes feel because of this she must be in the wrong

This should not be too difficult for a steady hand.

business but she so obviously loves it that she must be far tougher than she at first appears. She is fortunate in having a husband, Desmond, who adores her.

As we cruised along, I wondered aloud if the setting stirred any memories of the lakes and mountains of her homeland, New Zealand. Her response was enthusiastic: 'Oh, complete childhood. It's wonderful. You just put your hand over the side and you can drink the water. That's what I used to do. I would say to my dad that I was thirsty and he would tell me to put a cup over the side and drink the water. Beautiful things like that. It's still here. It's still unpolluted. It's just divine.'

A 5-wood flies towards the 10th green at Loch Lomond and Dame Kiri looks quite satisfied.

I put myself off 30 handicap in terms of knowing opera, but it is an aspect of theatre that fascinates me. It can seem elitist, is often difficult to understand and the grandeur of the costumes sets it apart from other forms of music. Dame Kiri had a neatly considered response:

'I try very hard for it not to be elitist,' she said, 'and one way of encouraging people to come and see opera is to put up sub-titles or whatever and immediately those people who cannot understand the language we are singing in, have their interpretation. They suddenly feel as though they are part of the scene and that they understand every word we are saying. If you have that you stop people being separated from the opera and you encourage them. As for the costumes, well I think there is the fantasy of being kings and queens and being able to command that somebody be put to death or that there has been a murder or a conspiracy or the King of Italy has been secreted away and out through the tunnels. People are still overwhelmed by royalty and upper-crust people. The President of the United States is seen as a god and everyone bows to him. People love to be near power. And so people fantasize in opera and about being powerful and therefore it becomes strangely unreal.'

So how did Dame Kiri begin her career? 'I cannot really define where it all happened. All I know is that I was seen to be on one path and I was never allowed to stray from it by something within myself and something within my parents. From a very early age I knew that somehow I was devoted to music. Music had to be my life and I was never, ever, allowed to desert it. I felt that if I deserted music I would lose my reason for living almost. When I first started to sing I went to a nun. My parents moved me from my home town of Gisborne to Auckland. I went to Sister Mary Leo, a Sister of Mercy nun. She was a wonderful woman. I was a Catholic going to a Catholic school and I started learning from her at the age of fourteen. She had a wonderful way of being able to teach us. We were all in the choir and we all sounded the same. Her main contribution to me was the strengthening of my vocal cords and the muscles that enable me to sing for long periods. I don't think that she was particularly knowledgeable. In fact she was always saying that she was totally unorthodox in the way she taught us. But she seemed to have a good recipe for success.

'Now I just think about going on as long as I want to, as long as I love it. Somebody said that the vocal cords don't fail. It's the muscles around them. The muscles start to sag and that is important to know. Singing is an athletic business. You've got to be able to breathe and control the breath and make sure the breathing is in the right place. I also find that the older people get the more they say to me, "I keep losing my voice". Jackie Stewart said to me, one day, that he had a big seminar to do but that he kept losing his voice. I told him he was not breathing properly. I think you can sing for as long as you want but there is an elegant way to go about it.

'I just love tunes. You come to the end of a modern opera these days and – this is my favourite saying – "Does anyone come away singing the tune?" If they don't you think they are either unmusical or we haven't got the plot or there aren't any tunes. All I want to do today is just sing beautiful tunes and lovely words because it is a fantasy world and we are allowed to be lost in our little fantasies for a very short time. I love feeling good and singing and having wonderful orchestrations.

'The music is different today. The Broadway composers of the thirties, forties and fifties were literally churning out glorious words like a factory. 'Can't Help Loving That Man' and so on were just full of wonderful words. You've got to croon it away but you've not got to be silly about it. Either you can do it or you can't. I have done a lot of learning through this, and the better the arrangers I have, the better my chances of being successful.

'I love it. Eventually, I think everyone goes back to his or her roots. As much as I love Britain, and as much as I love being here in Scotland, which is just to die for, you have to return to your roots. There is something about your blood, coming to a stop, to cool down or whatever it does. Everyone comes back to their roots. They want to die where their roots are.'

For many, many more years one of the most beautiful voices in the whole world will be around to serenade us, whether it is in opera, the Songs of the Auvergne or those timeless standards from the great musicals. Why not, as a one-off, follow the three famous tenors, Pavarotti, Domingo and Carreras, with three sopranos? Or, I ventured, has that concept prostituted the profession?

'I do not think it has prostituted it. In some ways when an organization or a presenter does try to put something on without a good sound system or without a good orchestra in a nasty venue, I find *that* prostitutes it. I find that all audiences today want to go to something that is truly interesting at

OVERLEAF The good ship 'Marion' and Dame Kiri is off to help the Loch postman deliver the mail.

Another round over, now where's that single malt whisky they were telling me about.

Another good shot at Loch Lomond and Dame Kiri promises to play more often.

a nice venue. They don't want to go to something in a tin shed and then say, "It's awful, it's freezing and the car-parking is dreadful." You've got to tempt your audience to come to see you. But with the three tenors, that's a major recipe for success because there *are* only three. I've been asked, since their first concert, if I would do three sopranos and I asked them who they would choose. I could name fifteen. There are not three sopranos in the world as special as the three tenors. There are fifteen to twenty very, very good sopranos and selecting three would be extremely difficult.

'The three tenors are lovely guys, but in the end, just human beings who do extraordinary things with their voices.

'It's important that the public likes you, but if they don't they come to see fisticuffs. As you may have heard, lots of opera singers tend to fight a bit.'

Between themselves, you mean?

'Yes. It's a nasty world. It's quite vicious. You know, one management trying to oust another management's singer and things like that. As long as you don't take too much notice and do your job and stand up and be counted you'll be all right, I always say. But don't play games. I hate games.'

Perhaps it is the contentment of a happy marriage and two lovely adopted children that have made Dame Kiri the rounded, feet-on-the-ground person she really is. I asked how much she enjoyed parenthood.

She said: 'Either we have failed or we have succeeded. Most parents today would say that it is a no-win situation. I am very proud of my two children. They have never caused us a moment's worry. They have not done drugs. My daughter has done extremely well at school. They have been wonderful kids but I would not like to judge myself as a parent. It is very difficult being a parent who has a career. I have had massive support from Des. He has been absolutely wonderful and not many husbands would put up with what he has. You know, a lot of people try to befriend us for the wrong reasons. He can see them coming. He sees red lights and quickly decides if someone is not the right person for us. You asked me if I might go home one night, open a nice bottle of wine and say, "You know, Des, I think I've had enough of this caper." I've been saying that for the last seven years. There are so many things I would like to do. I love trout fishing. But, I promise you, what I'm going to do in the next very short time: I'm going to play golf. That's it.'

It was time to buy her a large one. As we strolled back to the big house it was not difficult to imagine the Colquhouns and MacGregors fighting over this beautiful landscape into which the golf course is so cleverly moulded; nor Mary, Queen of Scots, penning her love letters in the old castle. Now the large drawing room of Rossdhu is the main clubhouse where the tired golfer may take a wee dram, a sandwich or something more and by the end of 1997 Lyle Anderson, the owner, expects to have spent another £10 million creating more rooms and cottages. The drawing room is the centrepiece, a Colquhoun family portrait gallery. There are books, battered with age, and display cabinets of items from generations long gone. Either side of the huge fireplace hang two charming little pictures of the Winter King and his wife, Elizabeth of Bohemia, sister of King Charles I.

The sweet, smoky aroma of a log fire and a glass of single malt were welcome as the gentle light of a late Scottish afternoon gave a translucence to the water of the loch. Dame Kiri and Des left us to reflect on a perfect day. London's traffic seemed to exist on a different planet: in such a setting as Loch Lomond anyone's sense of wonderment would be enhanced. I mused to anyone who cared to listen, 'All this is like a magic carpet adventure. It's wonderful. This is not the real world.'

Outside a pheasant clucked in the woods. The deer were there but hiding. A heron was flying home. Take the high road or the low road, but make sure you arrive at Loch Lomond.

41

DESERT DREAMS COME TRUE

Take a stretch of inhospitable desert with its cactus, its red rock out-crops, its local population of rattlesnakes, and turn the wilderness into one of the most spectacularly luxurious golf courses in the world. That was the challenge that Lyle Anderson gave himself when he went to Arizona with money and dreams and created Desert Mountain. It is a sumptuous arrangement of four golf courses and a clubhouse with sculptures, paintings and furnishings that makes the visitor think that luxury is not a strong enough word. With Desert Highlands an older sister and Las Campañas in Santa Fe, New Mexico, a smart cousin, there was plenty of reward to be had in the golfing paradise of the south-west of the United States.

The sense of anticipation at the end of a long flight was enhanced by the knowledge that I was to meet, talk and play with Dan Quayle at Desert Mountain, Gene Hackman and Anderson himself at Santa Fe, and the man who went to the moon, Admiral Alan Shepard, at the Sedona Resort ninety miles to the north of Arizona. It would be hard to find a more interesting and diverse set of companions: Quayle, the former US vice-president; Hackman, the most compelling of actors; Anderson, the real-estate billionaire who started with nothing; and Shepard, the Top Gun pilot, who became a celebrated, yet understated, astronaut.

Along with the golf courses I visited, these men made it one of the most exciting golfing journeys imaginable. Perhaps we should begin at Desert Mountain, a complex of four magnificent courses all designed by Jack Nicklaus and home of The Tradition, the American Seniors event

The Scottsdale Princess, Arizona, the perfect hotel base for a golfing break.

that is regarded as one of the US Seniors majors and invariably brings together as many of the old masters as possible – Nicklaus, Arnold Palmer, Gary Player, Lee Trevino, Ray Floyd *et al.*

They play on the Cochise course and, with Geronimo, Apache and Renegade being the other courses, you can see that the old Indian theme has been preserved. It is graphically, but not overpoweringly, visible in the architecture and furnishings. On each of the courses, Nicklaus has managed to create something different.

Apache is the newest, opened in 1996. This covers 7300 yards at a par 72 and undulates rather gracefully through the desert terrain. You could call it a more traditional approach to golf in the desert. Not easy, naturally, but there is a gentleness about it with the land sloping only slightly here and there while the greens are excellent targets, almost as an extension of the fairways. They will also accept the bump-and-run shots and it is clear that Jack has devised a course on which players of every level of ability can enjoy themselves – provided they can master the occasional tricky uphill and downhill lie.

It does not surprise me that most visitors want to head for the Cochise course, which seems to capture most of the surrounding Sonoran desert beauty. At 7048 yards it is not massively long, in the manner of some Nicklaus courses, but it has been recognized in several American magazine polls for its quality and standards of maintenance. The scenery would fit wonderfully into any travelogue but the golfer should beware. Despite the seductive, soft, smooth slopes you must be on the ball with your second shots and with your putting. The mammoth stone outcrops may be a distraction but the hidden slopes on the greens soon concentrate the mind. Two of Cochise's most memorable holes are the par three 7th and the par five 15th. The double green for these two perches on an island is approached from two different directions.

If you like your golf to involve huge elevation changes, deep ravines and plateaux, then the Geronimo course is the place to be. 'This is the strong-looking course, with Cochise being the soft one,' said Nicklaus, and when you tackle the carries over deep ravines and canyons on the back nine you understand why. On the card the finishing hole, a par three of 160 yards, reads cosily enough. Then you stand on an elevated tee demanding a pinpoint shot over a rugged canyon to a two-tiered green, protected by sand bunkers at the front and rear. It is a hole as memorable as the mountains.

Renegade is the course for all men of all seasons. It was designed that way with multiple tees at each hole. From the back it stretches 7515 yards so the killers of the game can make it as challenging as their competitive heart's desire. Now, I would not like this to read as a free advertisement for the place but I am only being honest when I say that the clubhouse was redolent of the desert, the Indians and immense investment. That is hardly surprising when you realize that an essential part of the Desert Mountain ideal, as with other American developments, involves selling property adjacent to the complex to people who also buy the exclusivity of membership. The clubhouse atmosphere is enhanced inside by rich woods and imported limestone while the outside is of native sandstone, recalling, I was told, the architectural styles of the early people of the area – the Anasazi. One of the most delightful aspects of the whole set-up was to be able to watch the sunset from the open terrace before dining in a room surrounded by uninterrupted glass.

It was in these surroundings that I talked to Dan Quayle, a politician who is clearly as much at home on the golf course as he is in propounding

45

LEFT Dan Quayle, politician, ready to take on the golfing challenge of Desert Mountain with a giant saguaro cactus over my right shoulder.

OVERLEAF Desert Mountain club house, perched proud and luxurious, behind the 18th.

his forceful views on defending the values of faith, personal responsibility, entrepreneurship and, his aides tell you in print-out form beforehand, the issues of today and the challenges of tomorrow. Yes, there was a desire to talk about politics rather than an out-to-in swing or an involuntary slice. He served under George Bush, of course, which kept up the remarkable record he has maintained since he became the youngest ever US Congressman at the age of twenty-nine.

There were quite a few questions I wanted to ask Dan Quayle. Although the cartoonists frequently lampooned him, a great wave of euphoria swept across the United States when he and President Bush were voted into the White House, and then they were booted out without sympathy. It must all have been rather hard to swallow, I suggested. 'Of course it was,' he said. 'It was not expected. We didn't plan it. We worked hard to have the opposite result but the American people just happen to have a way, like they do in Britain, of showing up and voting. You can be ahead in the polls two or three weeks before the election but you still lose. Bill Clinton ran a good campaign. We congratulated him on that but what I found very surprising was that after the Gulf War, in which the United States, Britain and the Coalition were victorious over Saddam Hussein, George Bush's approval rating was close to 90 per cent. Unprecedented, yet on election day we got only 37 per cent. That shows that, in politics, like in life, things can change dramatically and very quickly.

'But I love politics. I've been in public service and public life most of my adult career. I have six presidential elections to go before I turn seventy-three which seems to be a bench mark for running for president these days. Bob Dole, as you know, was seventy-three when he ran for president. Ronald Reagan was seventy-three when he ran for re-election to the presidency in 1984, so God willing I've got a lot of great years ahead of me and in one of those elections I very well may run myself.'

Why, though, had the political correspondents and particularly the cartoonists been cruel? I remembered seeing a profile of him in the British *Observer* under the headline 'Will Bush's Blue-eyed Boy Grow Up?' The article talked of the abundant Quayle jokes, frequently told by commentators and fed us just one: 'What are the most scary words in the language? Dan, I'm not feeling well.' The commentators talked about this blue-eyed, blow-dried, handsome man and mentioned his current reading matter, a book entitled *Competitiveness: The Executive's Guide to Success*, and concluded that he seized the advice comprehensively.

Sitting in the sanctuary of that Desert Mountain clubhouse, a cold drink at his side, Dan Quayle confessed that he had been hurt by some of the caricatures, despite being from a newspaper family himself. He said: 'They weren't kind. They weren't fair but that is really past tense. There were a number of factors. One, they were surprised that I was the choice and I found out that when the national media are surprised they don't really like it very much. I was the junior senator from Indiana but I was also a conservative. Most of the national correspondents who cover presidential politics are my age, of the baby boom generation, but they are quite liberal and I think they were horrified at the prospect that a conservative would be the first on a national ticket and perhaps the first elected to national office, which we were, in 1988. There is a book that I wrote called *Standing Firm* in which I spent a great deal of time talking about the media, how they like to put out caricatures, fairly and unfairly, and just leave them there. You mention the political cartoonists. They are the bane of all politicians. They can really stick it to you in a very direct and painful way.'

Perhaps they were at odds with his bold thoughts on family values, abortion, life. I could not help wondering if the changing face of the world might have altered his opinions. Not a bit of it, and the very idea started a political monologue that took him from the Gulf War to Chechneya and back again.

He said: 'I started this conversation on family values back in the United States in May of 1992. At the time I was roundly and severely criticized. A lot of controversy and ridicule and abuse came my way. Since that time we have made full circle. We've come a long way because whether you are Conservative, Republican or Liberal Democrat we are talking about families and family values. As you look at the value issue you have to consider the broader picture: creating jobs and opportunities, reforming our education system and getting rid of the welfare state. Finally, there needs to be a recognition that this world of ours is still a very dangerous place. Russia has 50,000 nuclear weapons. They have had a difficult time controlling their military inventory in the

49

war against Chechneya. The Chechens get the equipment from the Russian military and then turn around and kill Russian soldiers. If the Russians cannot control their own inventory I wonder if they have control of all their nuclear weapons and stockpile. And if they don't, where are they? Does Iran have it? Does Iraq have it? Does Syria? Does Libya? Does one of those other rogue nations have a nuclear weapon? What if Saddam Hussein had the weapon of mass destruction when he invaded Kuwait? Would we have made the same decision? Would George Bush and Prime Minister Margaret Thatcher have agreed to the same coalition and the same military exercises? Fortunately we don't have to answer that question because we knew that he didn't but we also found out that he was on the road to getting it. So this world needs to have our attention. International affairs, foreign policy, very important.'

All of this may seem a world away from knocking a 9-iron to the heart of a green under the bright desert sun but it is not often you have a former United States vice-president, perhaps a future president, captive at the 19th. Bearing in mind that James Danforth Quayle could yet be America's great man of destiny there were some worthwhile questions to be asked. We would all like to know whose finger is on the American button. I asked him to consider if his country would become the nation to which the world looked for leadership and advice, as a century ago everyone looked to Britain.

His response had the ring of the natural politician when he said: 'We have absolutely no interest in building an American empire around the world. We do have a great interest in making sure there is local determination, democracy, and that human rights are abided by and we will continue to be in the vanguard and will try to be that flame of democracy around the world. But we have no interest in any kind of colonization programme. That is not in the American culture and it is not in our interests, but clearly America is a super-power in the world. Other countries look to America for leadership. We need to use our power and our influence in a judicious way. It has to be of respect and wisdom and I do not believe that building an empire would fit that category at all.'

As we talked on that soft, splendid afternoon with the sun dipping towards the peaks, our immediate world had an untroubled look about it. The golf courses were empty now and a gentle breeze teased the

Dan Quayle lines up a tricky putt at Desert Mountain's 18th.

51

flags. Perhaps it was this sheer, peaceful isolation that drew me towards some of the twentieth century's most depressing problems. Dan Quayle's passion for the warmth of family values made me recall their erosion through violent films, bad language, fornication. Where would it all end?

'There's not a lot that politicians or the Government can do about it,' he said, perhaps rather defensively. 'You cannot pass a regulation. You cannot come up with a law and get it implemented to bring about instant change. You can encourage producers of some of these shows to change. You can encourage those who are in the entertainment community to put out films that have a good moral taste rather than ones that simply debase our culture. But they have to recognize that we need their help and to appreciate where we are. In America today one third of our children are born into homes without fathers. Violent crime is increasing. Teenage suicide for those between fifteen and nineteen is the leading cause of death for those kids. We have kids today who graduate from high school but can't read the diploma. Our social pathologies of illegitimacy, of teenage violence, of criminal activity, or drug abuse are really hurting us and families. And when families are hurt your country hurts. That is the reason we focus so much on trying to rebuild and to strengthen the American family because America will be strong only if her families are strong, and right now her families are being challenged like never before.

'There is always going to be trash on television. There is going to be trash at the movies. The only thing you can say is, "Look, you are smart people, you love your families, you love your country, help us. We need help." Why not have a movie that glorifies marriage, for example, instead of always tearing it down? Why not have a movie or a television series that shows the important role a father plays in the family? That the father ought to be there, that the father ought to be involved with his children, that the father ought to go to parent-teacher meetings, that fathers are really quite relevant when it comes to the child's development. We need their help. Join the parade, join the crusade in trying to strengthen our families and helping America.'

The inevitable comparison between America and Russia has intrigued many people, over the years, and at no time more than the present, now that many of the old Communist barriers have been broken down. Did Quayle see similarities between the two nations?

'Not really, because Russia has always been oppressed,' he said. 'It's always had the Tsars before it had Lenin and Stalin and all those Communist dictators. Russian history is one that is undemocratic. The history of America has been one of total democracy. A representative democracy is the proper definition so from that point of view our paths are very different. Russia was a super-power only because she possessed nuclear weapons. Take those away and she is not a major power. She is always going to be important because of the great land area that she occupies – eleven time zones, just think of that.

'The people are really tasting democracy for the first time. They engaged in a democratic election in 1996. Hopefully, they will continue down the road towards full implementation of democratic values but I don't know. I don't know where Russia is going to go. We need to keep an eye on Russia because it has been so important strategically but I do not think there is much comparison. Any affinity is because the United States recognizes the importance of Russia. It is an important country but our cultures are very different.'

It was time for him to leave Desert Mountain and all its splendour. The conversation had been fascinating, and as we shook hands, I could not help mentioning that though he was currently on the fringe of politics I felt we had not seen the last of him as a world figure. Those political cartoonists may be cheered by his response: 'Probably not. I still consider myself a young man and, God willing, we've got a lot of great years ahead of us. We'll see.'

I was reluctant to leave Desert Mountain, with its elevated tees and soft, receptive fairways, its creature comforts within the clubhouse, its tennis courts, swimming pool, fitness centre, and go on to Santa Fe where Lyle Anderson, the man behind so many golfing dreams, and Gene Hackman were waiting. As we drove away from Desert Mountain's 8000 acres with 250 tawny-coloured homes nestled gently on the southern slopes of the Tonto foothills, a few words from Jack Nicklaus filtered through my mind. He had said: 'What Lyle Anderson has given us is unique. I call it a golf park that keeps the houses off the course. It is special. And the desert out here is just so beautiful, even I couldn't mess it up.'

Sedona, wonderfully attractive and even more so when you hit it close to the flag.

54

Someone like Anderson enthralls me as much as, I am sure, he does Jack. He came from nowhere, got into selling real estate after graduating from the University of Washington, with a degree in electrical engineering, and now runs an astonishing empire, including Loch Lomond in Scotland, with offices in Arizona, Washington, Hawaii and New Mexico. Everything he touches seems to turn to gold. He has a gift for turning bleak landscapes into stunning golf courses with expensive properties. He quickly lets you know that there were early days when times were hard. So hard, in fact, that soon after leaving college he had to borrow 600 dollars to buy a wedding ring and began selling real estate at weekends. He says he hit a lucky streak following the advice of a man he met along the way when he decided to put some money into land. He began with Desert Highland, a predecessor to Desert Mountain and Las Campañas but the challenges were similar.

He made it all sound easy when he talked about his and Jack Nicklaus's creations among the barrenness: 'First of all the desert looks more unfriendly than it is. It appears that way and scares a lot of people and there are certain conditions that you have to deal with but I don't know if building a course in the desert is any more difficult than building it in the trees. You don't have to clear and you don't have some of the drainage problems. We go round the big rocks. We try to design our golf courses to move around the elements of the desert. I think you saw that at Desert Mountain.'

The idea of all this work going on in virgin desert country made me fear for the safety of the workers: I was looking out of the window of the car when I spotted a four-foot rattlesnake meandering sedately through the car park close to the attractive adobe clubhouse (size 46,000 square feet, cost $12 million). 'They are slow,' said Anderson, with conviction. 'They are not aggressive. They are very timid and will warn you if you get close to them. They would rather have you stay away. We haven't had any accidents or problems and we have been developing in the desert for fourteen years.'

With a golf course that cost $10 million to build, miles of roads linking the housing and the installation of water and electricity, Las Campañas was just as impressive as Desert Mountain. Anderson, who got down to 2-handicap after playing baseball in college, bought his first major piece

of land in 1979 and called Jack Nicklaus in 1980 because, as he explained: 'I was impressed with Jack's excellence in everything he did. He had just designed Muirfield Village Golf Club which was becoming famous. We began working together then and started the development of the 860 acres of Desert Highland in 1982.

'We have designed a lot of different golf courses. I have started out at the very high end of the club market. Currently we are working on two private clubs that are going to be much more in the medium range for golfers. That is one of my objectives, to bring quality golf to a wider market. Quality is so much more fun to do. It is much more rewarding personally. The people who come out and play our courses really enjoy it. In the long run, all of us strive for quality in everything we do. It's our philosophy. Quality costs money but it is surprising how proper design and proper engineering do not cost as much as people think. You have to spend money to move some earth properly so that it really fits and is environmentally sound, but with creative and imaginative design you could make five or six golf courses in the same complex uniquely different from each other. Our goal would be to make different styles of bunkers, tees and greens, vegetation and terrain. We were fortunate in the Desert Mountain project. There was such a wide variety of terrain out there.

'It was very exciting. We broke ground there in 1985 and I had Jack Nicklaus design all four courses. He will be starting on a fifth soon. We went out on that Desert Mountain property and we found the different sites. We had a lot of fun designing those courses and I think we accomplished our goal. The courses all have unique personalities. I think Jack and I have built a business together. His design, and projects of mine, have worked well. He has been excellent to work with. I have total admiration for his ability. A lot of people don't realize how hard Jack works to build one of these golf courses and how involved he is and how much he is the real designer. He certainly has some help with engineers and associate designers because he cannot be here all the time. But he made fourteen trips to Las Campañas and fashioned every green, every bunker and practically every roll on every fairway. Jack is talented.

'I have plans for a multi, five- or six- golf-course complex and I would like to use Tom Weiskopf as well as others. Arnie Palmer has been a good friend of mine for years and I would love to have Arnie do a golf course for us. I've talked to him about it and it would be a pleasure to work with him.

'We are not cavalier with money but I believe money follows quality and quality comes first. A lot of our organization is out in the future. We find that we are all trying to build quality but we try to make it enjoyable because at the end of the day money is not the most important thing. It's what you do with your life. It's the journey we are on.'

Maybe that enjoyment, that comfort on the journey through life, was reflected in the Santa Fe clubhouse. It cast all the right reflections of life in New Mexico, the state they love to call the land of enchantment. They will lull you with descriptive overtures about the sierra canyons and the music of the fluttering aspen leaves.

They will say that the clubhouse captures contemporary life in a historic way; that it evokes the narrow paths, the Navajo blankets, the seductive sculptures, pottery and paintings all blending with the Sangre de Cristo mountains on the horizon. You could not argue, especially when Anderson is saying: 'This was a labour of love for all of us. We completed in September 1996. There is a very well-known artist and designer called Bill Paul, whom I have known for years and who specialized in this kind of Santa Fe architecture. I asked Bill to be the designer and we had other people, landscape architects and interior designers and got a team together to build this but Bill was the lead designer. He has the touch for this style and I hear that it is the biggest adobe building to go up in the United States in the last sixty years. The mud bricks are authentic. That does cost a bit more but it has a lot of character. I get involved with some of the things directly. Others I just oversee but we did this by committee. There may be half a dozen people on the committee and sometimes they get outvoted six to one. Most of the time we try to stay democratic. I think you should model your club today on what the members would like to have. We should listen to that. They are the ones who are paying their way to be members of the club.

'I see us continuing to focus in the south-west. It's a great market. It's a growing area and we are well established here. After a while we are going to have a fairly significant portion of our business here. That does not rule out the possibility of a Loch Lomond type of club.'

57

Las Campañas, and the biggest adobe club house in America. Inside was impressive, too.

Ah, Loch Lomond, that jewel north of Glasgow. Why Loch Lomond? How did he come by it? And what are his plans?

He said: 'Tom Weiskopf and Jay Morrish designed the course and Tom is a good friend and neighbour of mine and he kept after me. Then Brian Morgan, one of the well-known golf photographers from Scotland who was also on at me, told me that the Bank of Scotland was about to sell it. They had had to repossess it and so I went over and had a look. I am very pleased with it. It is one of the most exciting things I have ever been involved with. We have an international membership that is growing every day. We are trying to have a golf club that promotes world-wide camaraderie with peoples from everywhere. We are evolving the Loch Lomond World Invitational within the European Tour.

'We are going to build some overnight accommodation for our members and so have the flavour of an international golf club so that people can come from all over the world and stay and play golf and bring their friends and enjoy their time. It is not true to say that we have not encouraged local Scottish members, which is a charge that has been levelled at us. We have several local members. To have an international course we need local members as well. Obviously, if we have too many local members there would be no room for the international members. We have been trying to organize our membership programmes.

'With Las Campañas, Desert Mountain and Desert Highlands, the only way to join so far is to purchase real estate because we needed that income to finance the golf and other activities. Loch Lomond has no real estate with it, just a membership and a club with overnight accommodation. We will build cottages and so on. We are just building the club and feeling our way and trying to decide the direction of the club through experience.

'One thing we have decided is that we are going to limit play on our courses to fifteen thousand rounds per year. There will be two courses so that we can maintain the wonderful quality of experience you get at Loch Lomond and it will never be crowded.'

At all of Anderson's courses you can be sure of good taste and valuable artefacts. The notions of the best interior designers seem to have worked in every room. The wonderful selections of paintings at Las Campañas focus on local Indian, cowboy and western art forms and some of the sculptures are quite staggering. In Scotland the quality is just as rich with some ancient books four or five inches thick. He said: 'I picked some of them through an auction. We are always interested in old books. If anyone has something they would like to show us I would always be interested. I love the history of golf and the history of that area around Loch Lomond. It's just fascinating. We are going to name the trophy for the World Invitational, which is in the form of a replica of the manor house, the Sir James Colquhoun Trophy. He was head of the clan when the house was built. There is a big picture of Sir James in the drawing room. He was quite a character. We are renovating the main house. Downstairs will be the locker room and a spike bar. Upstairs will be wonderful dining rooms, the drawing room, bar and a members' private room at the back. It will be a traditional clubhouse kind of thing. It is not a short term type of thing. We are looking at it over the next ten, twenty, thirty years.'

Somehow the conversation had strayed away from the desert and mountains of Arizona but we were soon back at Las Campañas for a dinner that matched everything about the style of the place. Take note of this fare served in the clubhouse's Hacienda restaurant: oak-whiskey-barrel smoked salmon with roasted *poblano*, fresh horseradish, capers and bruschetta, followed by a house salad of field greens tossed in balsamic vinaigrette with roma tomatoes, cucumber, feta cheese and kalamata olives. After that there was a choice of oven-poached Atlantic salmon fillet (in tomato saffron broth with seared wild greens and New Zealand green lip mussels) or aged Black Angus New York steak (with wild mushrooms and bourbon reduction) or Dijon crusted rack of lamb (three-peppercorn sauce and roasted shallot and rosemary mashed potatoes). The crême brûlée with home-made cookies made an exquisite dessert and the wines were engrossing, too. No haggis here.

The following day it was time to meet and play one of the locals at Las Campañas. His name? Gene Hackman – and it would take an entire chapter to list the films and awards that have gone his way in the last quarter of a century. You will surely remember *Bonnie and Clyde*, *The French Connection*, *The Poseidon Adventure*, *Mississippi Burning*, *Postcards from the Edge*, the Superman films and many more. These days he is a gloriously relaxed member of the Santa Fe community, golfing, painting,

61

walking and wondering if the time is close when he might no longer be attracted back to Hollywood. He is an intensely private man, not really in love with the idea of fame or the so-called glamour of the movie business. But he feels a strong pull to the golf course. His golf, I sensed, was not to be taken too seriously. It seems he was making a film with 20th Century Fox in Los Angeles just across the road from the prestigious Riviera Club. As he said, in his classic, laid-back way, he 'just went over there one day and took a club and started whacking it around and really enjoyed it'.

Perhaps there was a little more to it than that but as we were about to go out and play I needed to know something about the opposition. You quickly discover that Mr Hackman is master of the understatement. He said with the kind of drawl that would have been appropriate to his 1994 film *Wyatt Earp*: 'I've taken lessons a number of times from a variety of people. The last time was with Jim Flick with whom Jack Nicklaus had an association. That was good because they have a class and you share with ten or twelve people so there's a bit of dialogue and it isn't just a one-on-one thing where you burn out. Knowing that we are going

Gene Hackman relaxes in his 'Cafe Escalera' in Santa Fe.

to play later today I don't know if I should tell you my strengths and then have to eat those words. I suppose the short irons would be it. I have an arthritic wrist from time to time. It acts up and I don't hit the long ball too well. I would love to. I think everybody does. I don't play regularly because I have been working so much for the last four or five years. When I am in LA I play with a couple of friends at public courses. I like that. In California there are some good public courses and the fellow I play with knows a couple of people so we get to play at some of the country clubs but we just laugh a lot. That, for me, is what it is about. Just getting out and laughing and having a good time.'

Gene Hackman has given the people of the world much pleasure through the silver screen for nearly three decades and I had to ask him how it all started and how he felt about the current trends towards violence and the apparent need to shock.

He said: 'I don't recall what the first movie was but I was always taken with James Cagney and Errol Flynn and some of the guys who had a bit of style. To this day I still think that Cagney is one of the best-ever film actors. It's true some of the things he tried did not work. Some of his Westerns were laughable, but he was a wonderful actor and had a lot of energy. He was just full of life. I suppose they were a bit corny in those days but when you get to my age [sixty-six] you think back to what we were being entertained with. There was not a lot except, perhaps, the movie once a week. They were certainly gentler. You wouldn't have the big, violent films that you have now. There was violence but it was not as graphic as it is now. We didn't see blood. There was a censoring arm in the motion-picture business and you could not fire a gun and see the victim in the same shot. You could only see the gun and then you had to cut away to see the victim. What that did, I don't know. That was their idea of tempering some of the violence. There is a big controversy today about whether violence in films carries to the outside world and affects young people. Do people do violent acts after they have seen a film? I suppose some do ape what they have seen on the screen. Young guys want to be cool. A certain kind of actor might be cool and handle weapons and that sort of thing. I suppose some of it's bad. But there has always been violence in the theatre; in *Lear*, in all the Shakespeares. They were full of violence and we all love murder-mystery. We just love that. I don't know why. We like the scariness. We go to films and watch television to be frightened, I suppose, to be titillated.

'I was in the theatre first. I was in New York for twenty years and did a number of Broadway shows. I loved the theatre. I went back a couple of years ago after being off the stage for twenty years, and from time to time somebody will ask me to go in and speak to young people, at university or whatever, about acting and I generally answer questions. One of the questions that is always being asked is: "What is the difference between stage acting and film acting?" I have often said there isn't any real difference. But after going back and experiencing the theatre again I have to revise my thinking.

'I had forgotten how much energy and concentration and dedication it took once you are on stage to sustain a performance for two and a half hours or so. It was difficult. You have to project, and as soon as you start to project things become a bit false. It is very easy to be the real you if you can be small the way we are in films, and modulate down. In the theatre you can't do that. You have to be heard a hundred and fifty feet back.'

I sensed that, successful though he constantly was, Hackman was not entirely happy with the actor's life. Sure, the money was good, but I suspected that he would be happier without the bright lights and constant exposure.

He has his own theory: 'One of the things that was attractive about the business as a youngster was the seemingly glamorous idea of the movie or television coverage of the Academy Awards and that kind of thing. You would see those beautiful people all dressed up and it seemed like it would be fun to go along with, just doing what you longed to do, to act.

'Once I got involved with that in California, after I left New York and Broadway, I realized after a short time that it wasn't really why I was in the business at all. I wasn't any good at that. I really felt uncomfortable with it. I don't put people down for loving it. It takes all kinds to make the world go round. I just realized that I was good at what I did, let other people get on with their thing, and have as little of that business to deal with. I loved doing my acting and coming back here to Santa Fe and not having to deal with that glamorous world. It's false but it's a necessary world. You have to have a lot of child in you in order to do this business because it's a kind of delving into your mysterious self and asking, "Is this real what I'm doing? Is this fantasy?" You keep going back and forth all the time. There's reality there and there is this fantasy to create. The average guy in the street wouldn't want to do that. He could maybe do it for a day or so and then say, "Hey, I don't feel like doing this." It takes a certain kind of person who loves acting and loves the fantasy to do that. It's fine to have that fantasy going for yourself while you're doing it but you need to be able to cut it off and a lot of people never manage to. They live in that kind of unreal world where you need a lot of back-slapping and bolstering and a pat on the rump every once in a while.'

Hackman leaves the partying to Hollywood and comes home to the desert hills, where he has lived for ten years, and indulges in his great passion for painting and sketching

Strong grip, gentle swing and Gene Hackman is not acting.

which, he says, is for his own entertainment and gratification and not for selling. Clearly, he is a man who abhors first nights, does not want to be dressing up in his tuxedo and drinking sherry in the cocktail circuit. He is attracted to the open air and the big sky of Arizona. He has his own ways of escaping.

As he put it: 'This is an unusual town in that there are thirty art galleries and we have a real class opera and a chamber orchestra. There are lots of things to do here. You would think it's just desert but I consider it the high desert, which means it is cooler than, say, Arizona. There are

mountains right by and wonderful restaurants. There are six or seven really top restaurants in Santa Fe that would do any city proud. The town is full of writers so that although we are away from the business there are still a lot of artistic and very bright people here. I don't go downtown a lot. I suppose I could go down into the square and sign autographs or something like that. People don't recognize me a lot of the time. There is a way to carry yourself where if you want to be recognized you will. And there is a way you can just be a person and go about your business. Wear a cap and glasses and that's fine.'

For all his love of Santa Fe privacy and his escapes from 'the business' there is no doubt that Hackman remains a prolific worker. It made me anxious to know whether he was driven by impressive story lines or a more fundamental and basic need to keep earning money. He says: 'The money is great. We certainly make more money than we are worth, probably, but there is a kind of love of doing what I do. It's hard to describe, really. When I'm actually doing it, actually saying the words, actually in a scene with someone, that to me is the best thing that can happen. As soon as it's over, from then until the time I do it again, you know it's hell because the business for me, the showbusiness kind of thing, that's difficult for me. I don't like that. I don't deal well with people who are involved in that. I tend not to be very diplomatic about all that – I suppose because I started in the business thinking I was going to be an artist and an actor.

'When you have to deal with these very tough businessmen and turn right round and start a sensitive scene, that to me is hard. That would be hard for anybody but some people handle it better than others.

'You asked me which, of all the different kinds of dress I have worn throughout my movies, from modern suit to cowboy clothes, would I prefer, say, for one last film. A military uniform pulls you right up and gives you the part of the character. Other things have a different effect. In a tuxedo you stand a little differently. I would say that if I had only one film left I suppose I would go for a military costume. It's not important to have plenty of ribbons and medals but it might be fun. I think one of the nicest uniforms I ever wore was that of the French Foreign Legion in a picture no one ever saw but I loved that costume with its funny little pill-box hat and so on. But I have played all sorts of roles. I

Gene Hackman, classic bad guy in many a film and a bit of a rascal with the putter here at Las Campañas.

67

love doing different types of thing. In the early days of live television in New York I did a variety of things. I was playing in a tuberculosis sanatorium one time, an ex-prize fighter who was a very soft, gentle guy.

'There are times now when I would like to stop. It's funny, when you get a little older you start to think in terms of your career and immortality and all that and how you want to be seen and remembered. I would not like to hang around and do small parts. I would rather stop when I am still offered the leads in films and feel like I have the energy to do them well. So probably in the next year or so. . .

'The business is so seductive. They keep offering you better roles and more money and more exotic locations, so it's tough to stop. My wife and I want to paint and walk and sail. I really like sailing, I'm not a great expert at it but we feel we can learn to do it well enough to be able to live on a boat for six months or so. It would be a sailboat. The Caribbean is at the back of our minds. You feel you'd like to do Tahiti some time. It would need to be a fifty- or sixty-footer. We wouldn't do a crew. We did that once before. We had an eighty-foot motor sailer and had a crew of three but it was all about them. They were having a great time but we didn't enjoy it much.

'Then, of course, we go up these mountains all the time. It's a wonderful place to hike, with all the great pine trees and beautiful aspen and lots of wonderful trails. My wife is a great photographer and always has her little Leica with her. I wouldn't call myself a photographer but I do love to paint. I suppose my style now would be kind of impressionistic.

'Rather like the French Impressionists, I suppose, but I would like to evolve into a more abstract painter. It's very difficult, though. I was trained as a commercial artist but I never worked at that. It was a very representational kind of training and difficult to move from that into the abstract. You know, I honestly cannot tell you how abstract painters see things because I haven't done enough of it. Abstract painting in some ways is more about shapes, just a shape or form or colour as opposed to trying to represent an object. The skill intrigues me. I think that probably a lot of people evolved into abstract painting because after you have developed a certain amount of skill in representing something you wonder how you can then represent it in a way that will have a more emotional effect on someone.'

Gene Hackman's sensitivity came through strongly during our talk at the golf club and later at a restaurant in the town. I wondered if, when shooting a particularly emotional scene, he had ever been overcome by words that trigger something inside him. He was delightfully honest: 'Yes, I have, and I always find it fascinating because I always work with a sense of relaxation. The older I get the more I am able to relax within the context of a scene. I was doing a scene recently with a young man and playing a very unattractive character. We were in the scene and talking about my daughter. Somehow or other, I was relaxed enough to be able to think about my own life in the scene. My daughters are not in any trouble but I connected with the character talking about his daughter in the movie and my own daughter, and I just started weeping. I kept doing the dialogue and the other actor just didn't know where this was coming from. It felt good. I just let it happen. It was no big deal. I don't know if they'll use it in the film but it felt right. Sometimes you choose, because of the way you are taught, to make it a deliberate choice to have an emotional response in a scene. Sometimes it doesn't work because you may be pushing too hard. But if you become relaxed enough and are able to fit your reaction to some emotional stimuli in the scene then you can make it happen for you.

'I've been very lucky. Very fortunate. I've done everything I've wanted to do. I had a lot of dreams and I've fulfilled them all.'

One thing he was especially sure about was that if he ever retired from acting he would never become a director. He said he could live without the need to work with people. 'I am not anti-social but artistically I am very stubborn. When I have been in trouble in films, and I have been in trouble a number of times, it is with what I suppose people would call temperament. When I am arguing or having fights with a director it is always with what I'm meant to be doing rather than the size of my trailer and how can I get out of this scene what I want from it. Sometimes you can't have that kind of conversation with the business people in movies. It's an impossible conversation to have and I don't think I would do that very well.

'So, we'll do a lot of hiking and camping out, tent and everything. We are outdoors people. We have two German shepherd dogs that we love. I'll do a lot of sketching, play some golf and take one or two of the

69

painting classes we have here in Santa Fe. Each day will start with some exercises, lifting weights or the treadmill. My wife is much better at it than I am. We're building a new house and we are often up, looking at that. It's closer to town yet more isolated with big trees and a lot of rocks around.

'There's about fifty acres. The terrain is too rugged to have horses but we've built a trail around the holdings of about two and a half miles so that if we want a morning constitutional it's there.

He seemed contented away from the business that made him famous though not quite as relaxed as the amazing Admiral Alan Shepard, who greeted me ninety miles north of Phoenix, Arizona, saying that he was puzzled that the British Flat Earth Society had not asked him to be a member.

Sedona Golf Resort is set among red rock cliffs where the views are nothing less than stunning.. Pines, aspens and cactus decorate a landscape that seems scarcely to have been disturbed by the installation of the par-71 golf course of 6646 yards from the back tees. There is water on six of the holes, including the last three which makes it a memorably tough finish. The 18th can be driven with a favourable wind but there is a long 'beach' bunker to the left of the approach to the green and a vast expanse of water beyond that. Both have been known to take merciless toll, ruining many a card. Perhaps a 3-iron from the tee and a pitching wedge might be the right idea. Admiral Shepard thought so, and you could never accuse him of over-caution: he was taken, after all, from fighter squadron to rocket ship where he clocked up 216 hours and 57 minutes in space. He is seventy-three now and looks nothing like it.

He graduated from Annapolis and began his naval career on a destroyer in the Western Pacific during World War II. He received his wings in 1947 and went on to become an aircraft carrier pilot and later a test pilot and instructor. He was the first American to journey into space in May 1961, but it was his landing on the moon that captivated the world, as he and command module pilot Stuart A. Roosa and lunar module pilot Edgar D. Mitchell made their way to the moon's surface. They carried out several tests and collected 100 pounds of lunar samples.

When you are in the company of a man who has achieved so much, golf is liable to seem trivial but Shepard was competitive enough to make

Admiral Alan Shepard took a 5-iron to the moon. Sedona was a different challenge.

71

sure that did not happen. His story is of a normal, young high school lad progressing through the usual channels until he found himself in the role of the man in the moon.

When he was at high school he worked part-time at the local airport for pocket money. He remembered his father talking to a former graduate of the Naval Academy about what his son might do when he left high school. He heard the friend say: 'Well, he's a smart little guy. Maybe he could pass the entrance exams and get an appointment and become a naval aviator.' That, he told me, was how it happened.

But there must have been more to it than that. I recall reading books on the war and the Battle of Britain and how some fighter pilots had quicker reactions, better hand-eye co-ordination and fired off the bullets more quickly. I wondered if he had some sort of inner balance that set him apart from the others.'There was a basis in that I was interested in aviation,' he said, 'but it was also a challenge to me. My life has been a series of challenges, one after another, each one being a little more difficult and a little more challenging than the previous one.'

As with all brave men and women, there is an endearing modesty about Admiral Shepard, whether he is talking about his early days as a test pilot or preparing to be fired into space. Did he never think, when he was testing planes that had never been up before, of the danger? Did it ever occur to him that he might not come back?

'It crosses your mind many, many times,' he said. 'And you adopt an attitude all the way through the process. What do I do if it doesn't work? What are my back-up schemes? Can I bale out? Can I eject? What do I do to overcome some kind of difficulty? Same thing in the space programme. It's a very deliberate, studied, disciplined approach to test flying airplanes and flying rockets. Going into the space programme, of course, we had been upside down as much as we had been right side up, and the physical manoeuvre was nothing new to us. The nose cone didn't look much like an airplane in that we wanted it to fly like an airplane. That was our challenge – to prove that pilots had a place in a nose cone in space. It was very, very manoeuvrable.'

I had always been amazed by the ease of communication in space flight and Shepard confirmed that their simulation on the ground was so good and so frequent that while they were orbiting it seemed as though they were talking to the guys next door. All the time, he said, they were developing ways of dealing with emergencies in a way that built up confidence. As we talked in the unlikely setting of the Sedona resort – unlikely only in that Shepard was telling a story that seemed like science fiction – I mentioned how well, fit and normal he looked. Some astronauts or cosmonauts had returned to earth as different men. Some had died, others, it was rumoured, had committed suicide, yet he seemed to have come sailing through.

He said: 'I think to generalize about chaps who have been to the moon and been in space and become famous because of that may be off key but the generality would be that each of us had a little difficulty in coping with becoming a national hero overnight. We were basically pilots dedicated to the job of going to the moon and back. You are satisfied when you come back, knowing you have done a good job. But with all this adulation and attention and so on some of the chaps had difficulty. Fortunately it was only temporary. A couple of the boys were rather religious before they went. They came back from the moon talking in more spiritual terms than some of the rest of us did. But, in general, the problems they have had have been because of the publicity and attention and in every case everyone has recovered well.'

Just as I was wondering if any abnormal reaction could be related to standing on the moon and looking down upon the earth he stopped me and said: 'That is a totally different process. I am glad you brought that up. Sure, after we landed on the moon we took emergency samples and we did our emergency things in case we had to lift off quickly. Then we had a rest period. I stood on the surface of the moon with the sun shining on the surface. The surface is lighted but the sky is totally black, no reflection, no diffusion because there is no atmosphere at all. And looking up at that black sky you see something which is much more than a pea-sized planet. It has colour, beautiful blue shades from the oceans, white from the ice caps of the North and South Poles and the outlines of continents in some cases when the weather is relatively clear. I stood there looking and it was a very emotional thing for me, saying that planet is finite. Down here we think it is infinite. You look at it from that distance and you can put it between your two fingers and say, "Hey, this thing has finite measurements and we've got to start thinking

OVERLEAF The red rocks of Sedona give the impression of belonging to another planet.

73

of taking care of it in the years ahead." From space you can see the Great Wall of China but not from the moon. From an orbit of four or five hundred miles above the surface you can see that. If you are in a relatively low orbit, say a couple of hundred miles, you can see the office buildings of downtown Phoenix or the office buildings in New York. It depends on the visibility, the weather and all kinds of functions.

'There is always a sense of nervousness when you are lifting off on the rocket or when you are actually slowing down and going into orbit around the moon or coming in to touchdown. Not because you are concerned about a failure, you practise for failure, but you are concerned that you might make a mistake if you have a failure.'

It occurred to me that we should be discussing his potent 12 handicap and the sheer, relaxing pleasure of the Sedona resort but I felt an irresistible urge to bombard him with more questions about his job as a NASA astronaut. Had it just been a race with the Soviets?

'There was a race,' Shepard said. 'The Cold War was still part of the lives of the Soviets and part of the lives of the Americans. There was a sense of competition. In the early days they did better because their missiles to launch their atomic warheads were much more powerful than ours because their warheads were larger. But when we designed Saturn V for the moon trips we took the lead because it was a missile specifically designed for the mission. The Soviets tried it and their design just didn't work.'

But had it been worth while? All those billions of dollars?

'It's a very difficult story to tell but I will give you one example,' he said. 'Look how much we depend on computers these days. Look how much we depend on communication satellites. The speed of computers today, the complexity of computers in these little packages – it's all because of the amount of money NASA spent in the mid-sixties when we had to design a computer to take us to the moon and back.

'They put the pressure and the money into the industry to make it happen. So many good things have happened over the years that the average individual doesn't realize that the technology he has today came from the space programme. Not a single dollar went to the moon. It went into the pockets of the people who worked on the programme, who built the craft, who built the rockets. Who sent us up there and brought us back, producing the kind of basic research that eventually meant products for the world today.'

How had he felt in that moment when he finally stepped out on to the moon? Was it as he expected? What was the surface like? Was there a possibility he could have been struck by a meteor?

'Well, of course we had some pretty good data,' Shepard said, matter-of-factly. 'There was photographic data taken from some unmanned probes as well that showed us the entire surface was pretty well covered in dust. In some places the dust was relatively thin and in others it had drifted up against the rocks. When a meteor comes in, as dozens of them do on the moon, and blows the dust around it tends to drift. We were not sure how deep the dust was going to be so we over-designed the huge pads on the bottom of our landing gear so that we wouldn't sink into it once we had landed. Other than that, not too many surprises. The flight before mine had actually photographed my site. We had scale models of the craters and so on and when I pitched over and looked at it from about ten thousand feet for the first time it was already a familiar place. Not too many meteors have come in during the last thousands of years. Micro-meteorites, pieces of dust and so on, keep hitting the surface and they are the ones that keep churning it up.

'It was a very satisfying part of my life. There was a great sense of personal satisfaction. Having been grounded for six years between flights it was marvellous to be able to overcome that and actually walk on the surface of the moon. I think I matured with the success.'

The golf course was having to wait as I quizzed him about UFOs and the ill-fated Challenger that blew up on take-off.

The Admiral said: 'I cannot help but believe that somewhere in this vast, vast universe of ours, with millions and millions of light years and dimensions, there is some other planet that has similar conditions to ours where people have lived with perhaps the same degree of intelligence. I just don't think we have seen any evidence of it here. I have a problem as to why somebody should come from millions and millions of light years away to land on this particular, puny planet just because there are no signals or lights coming from it. Why would they pick on

77

'I like the roll on these Sedona greens so much I think I'll keep the Odyssey putter.'

78

this one? That is the problem I have. But there's got to be life out there somewhere.

'I was in the control tower in Houston when Challenger exploded. It was a tremendous surprise obviously. There was an immediate sense of loss. How could it possibly happen? The mechanical problem was pretty well defined and corrected after a few weeks but all of us asked ourselves how could we, totally dedicated people, let this happen?

'Then you say to yourself, if you take Challenger, if you take the fire, that is two accidents in more than a hundred manned space flights. That was far better than was ever predicted. On the other hand you had to say that perhaps there was a sense of over-confidence. We had been totally successful with Mercury and Gemini. We were on our way with

79

Admiral Alan Shepard often looks up and says 'Yeah, I've been there.'

Admiral Alan Shepard (right) and Dan Quayle meet up for a chat at Desert Mountain.

Apollo and, boom, we have a fire. We are back on track but there is still a learning process when you have a fire.

'Do you know, I still look at the moon and give it a little "Yeah, I've been there." The beauty of the moon is just as attractive to me as it is to other people. But I think of the time when we had a few failures on the way out which could have precluded a landing. I think about looking back at the earth and how beautiful it was. I don't always think the same thing but there is always that sense of quiet, personal satisfaction in that I've been there and done that.'

When we finally teed up the ball on Sedona's opening par four hole you could see in every shot Shepard played the determination and pride of a rare human being.

81

THE TIN-MINER'S DIAMOND

There is a captivating, haughty mystique about Spain, as though the land was created for the grandees, matadors, painters, operatic singers and flamenco dancers who have shaped its elegant tapestry. The ancient city of Seville, where we began our visit, seems to have glided through the centuries maintaining just such a mystique but unfortunately we had to leave it behind as our main purpose lay on the Costa del Sol, a few miles east of the Rock of Gibraltar: Valderrama is the venue for the 1997 Ryder Cup and the multi-million pound pride and joy of Jaime Ortiz-Patino, 'Jimmy' to his friends, the scion of a wealthy Bolivian tin-mining family, and always so much in charge that he maintains all committees should be of an odd number and that three is too many.

This alluring country holds much more than golf courses. While I was there they were treading the grapes at Jerez. Deep in the isolated country-side an articulate young matador was demonstrating that even a training session could involve death in the afternoon. And to top it all we were joined by two contrasting visitors, the Olympic rowing gold medallist Steve Redgrave and a Russian politician, Alexsandr Pavlovich Vladislavlev.

Valderrama is the tin-miner's diamond: Patino has spent more than $35 million of his own fortune on the sculpting of what he hopes will be recognized as the Augusta National of Europe. He has bunkers at the back of the 17th to make it look like the 12th at Augusta and the front is designed to resemble the 15th on that great American course. There is much to commend Valderrama and there are some stiff holes that will be decisive when the Ryder Cup takes place. It also has its drawbacks:

Valderrama: home of the 1997 Ryder Cup and pride and joy of Jaime Ortiz-Patino.

Master of all he surveys at Valderrama, Jaime Ortiz-Patino.

the 12th, for instance, is a par three that is at least a 3- or 4-iron but with any wind you would require a wood for a very small target. The par five fourth, with its tight green and tumbling waterfalls, is undeniably spectacular but I am not convinced that it is a good par five. Why not make it a 475 yards par four so that they are all going for it?

Jimmy Patino is a roundly built man, always welcoming but, I suspect, a demanding perfectionist. I was interested to know how he arrived at Valderrama, what made him embark on this life's work and what goes on within the boundaries of this golf course with its slick greens, its water and wildlife sanctuaries. We sat together on the terrace of the Moorish clubhouse, sipping orange juice under a warm September sun, as we talked.

It had all begun like this, Patino said: 'I originally came for a holiday. I drove here from Geneva in a Ferrari and the roads in those days were not good. When I got to Marbella I nearly stopped because the road was getting worse. From Marbella until I got here there wasn't a single house except for the little fishing villages. There wasn't a construction. There was no grass. It was all brown. I was with a friend and I said, "We must have made a mistake and got on the wrong road." Then suddenly I came round the corner and I saw this oasis of green. It was Sotogrande. I fell in love with the place. There were eleven houses, a golf course, bungalows and nothing else in the whole place. Today there are fifteen hundred houses, two thousand bungalows and lots of people.'

Between times he played golf at Sotogrande, which was owned by Joe McMicking, a colonel in the American Air Force, who then built a second course that was to become Patino's own, Valderrama. He charted the route to ownership in his own way: 'They built this course here and brought in Henry Cotton to run it. He had just been thrown out of Portugal in the revolution and set up a school and began to give lessons. I came up to play a couple of times but it was difficult. It was very rudimentary. Every time you hit a fairway you bounced out of bounds, more or less. It was a nightmare. The greens were rock hard because they were never watered. It was not a lot of fun. Eventually Henry went back to Portugal and Tony Jacklin came on the scene. I heard that McMicking had passed on Sotogrande to his nephew and that they were in the process of selling things off. I heard the golf course was for sale and there was talk of a Butlin's holiday camp. I thought that would be the end of Sotogrande so I got together a group of friends and said "Let's buy it." I wanted to make it a real championship course because I like good things.'

With seven partners he set about transforming Valderrama and spent so much money that the other seven were happy for him to buy them out in 1989. He continued to chip away at the lay-out and create new irrigation systems, and insisted on nature conservancy. He said: 'Golf has got a bad name from the ecologists. I don't mind saying that this Spanish Green Party is more Communist than green. I call them the water-melons because they are green on the outside but red inside. They cannot wave the Communist flag any more so they wave the green. They are anti-golf because it is looked upon by many people out-side Ireland and the United Kingdom as élitist. There is even an anti-golf movement in Japan. It is absolutely wrong because here we have a haven for wildlife.

'We have possums, we have an eagle owl, we have buzzards, ospreys, foxes, badgers and all sorts of butterflies and small birds on this golf course. If you look at the hills, everywhere is brown because the cows have eaten everything. There is nothing, no life. We have areas on the golf course that are wonderful for nature. If this wasn't here, what would it be? Apartments, houses, a shopping centre. It must be better to have a golf course.'

No argument there. But one or two arose when the time came to allocate the 1997 venue for the Ryder Cup. The event had been played only once in Scotland, at Muirfield in 1973, and never in Ireland. Both countries have produced many players over the years and in the last decade Spanish players have also made major contributions to the game. I wondered how Patino had gone about bringing the great biennial match to the Costa del Sol.

OVERLEAF A quiet corner of Valderrama - one that will surely test the Ryder Cup players.

85

'First of all I had to find out why it had not come here four years previously. Seve Ballesteros had insisted that it should go out of England and into Spain because of what Spanish players had done and he did a lot for that. They had more or less agreed that the match would come to Spain but when the vote came down it was 3 - 3 and finally Lord Derby, who was chairman of the PGA, tipped the balance in favour of going back to The Belfry. One of the reasons that prompted them not to come to Spain was the proposed course – everybody knew it was Club de Campo, which is not a Ryder Cup course. I went to Kiawah Island in 1991. It was a terrible tournament for many reasons, not least because of the atmosphere. People were living an hour and a quarter away and being bussed in. I said that we had everything at Valderrama better than Kiawah. I said we had the golf course, better hotels, more courses. I said it was a better place and that if I could have land for parking, which Sotogrande will give me, I can do the Ryder Cup. Everything is all right now. We had difficulties in the beginning because of opinionated people who have their own ideas as I have mine. Today the relationship with the Andalusian government is very good, as it is with the Ryder Cup committee which is half PGA and half European Tour. We are getting on. I feel we can do it because I want it to be a success.

'As far as the course is concerned, when we come to the Ryder Cup what is important is the last four or five holes because we are in matchplay. They are outstanding finishing holes. The 14th, a par four, the 15th is the longest par three, and the 16th, has been described by people like Ronan Rafferty as the most difficult par four in Europe. Then there is the 17th, which we have rebuilt with Seve although it is a Robert Trent Jones course. He is ninety now and couldn't come here to do the 17th. He did every other hole but when we came to the 17th he said, 'Here's my sketch. If you are bidding for the Ryder Cup give it to Seve to do.' So Seve modified the sketch a bit. It is like the 15th at Augusta. If you don't land on the green you roll back in the water. It will make a fascinating hole because with no wind, or the wind behind, you can get on in two. I am happy with spectator movement around the course. Obviously this is not a stadium course. It is a course of beauty. At Oak Hill we could not get around the 14th and 15th holes yet they had the Ryder Cup there and it was a great success. We will overcome any bottleneck we may have here.'

There is no doubt that Patino is something of a dictator at Valderrama. He has a membership committee but nobody gets in without his approval. He once gave a serious finger-wagging lecture to a professional who left orange peel on the course. But he has a benign side. He realized that because there were no public courses in the area the local people and caddies would be deprived of playing the game he loved. He told the villagers they could play at Valderrama before the members went out on Saturdays, Sundays and holidays, and then decided that they should have their own nine-hole course. Robert Trent Jones gave the plans, Patino provided the irrigation and La Cañada was built next door, in the village of Guadiaro.

Patino sounds almost paternal as he says: 'Everybody worked on it and it's a fine course. Today everybody in the village plays. All the kids from four years on are up there hitting balls and the mothers are there, too. The football team was in the Third Division and playing well but it doesn't exist any more because they're all out playing golf. You have to have a public course to get people interested.'

But Valderrama is exclusive and, in Patino's words, it costs a lot of money to join. How much? 'It's private. I can say it doesn't cost as much as it does in Japan which may be $1 million in some clubs. In America if you want to join the Los Angeles Country Club it costs $125,000. It's not that much here. Basically you join here by invitation. People are introduced and I believe in a certain democracy although you say, "I am a dictator!" The admissions committee votes on any application and the majority rules. The only thing is that nobody can be put up to this committee unless I put them up. It has to come to me. I get introduced to them, I introduce them to members of the board. We try to have a round of golf and if he fits in well and knows the other members, that's all we want. We're not interested in handicaps but in people who mix well. I would like to have as members people I would like to have at my house and they would like to have me at theirs.'

Patino has an impressive collection of golfing artefacts. He is an avid student of sale catalogues and recently spent between two and three hundred thousand pounds at Sotheby's in London for a golf club and a painting. He says: 'I have been collecting all my life. My family collected and I collected things from snuff boxes to silver to books to furniture

It looks good in the air! But the roll was quick.

and Impressionist paintings. I go through phases and when I bought this golf course and we got into tournaments I said we should have some golfing memorabilia. I saw there were things on the market and that people were buying. I have quite a collection of Ryder Cup things but they will not be on exhibition until the match. Some things come up for sale, but I have paid a lot of money for things that did not come up for sale. The items I bought at Sotheby's I felt were needed for my collection. I bid quite a lot but I think they were worth it. I was lucky the Japanese were out of the market at that time because they buy anything at any price. Everything here is insured. We have security. The place is always under surveillance.'

At that moment, a giant of a man came round the corner of the single-storey clubhouse, a golf bag slung casually over his shoulder. It was Steve Redgrave, who has rowed in four successive Olympic Games and brought a gold medal home from each. He is a great man in every sense, constantly understated yet enveloped in an aura of strength and confidence. At six foot five and weighing more than sixteen stone he hits the golf ball a mighty distance. Yet he shows a deftness about the green which convinces me that if he ever really put his mind to the ancient game his 19 handicap would soon come tumbling down. The ninth at La Cañada requires a tee shot over a deep ravine, which has become the final resting place of many a golf ball. I was impressed with Steve's massive clearance but no more than I was with his deft 9-iron to within eight feet for his putt to shave the hole to a round of applause from a group of local children sitting by the bushes.

A par 3 at the difficult 12th. Most pros would settle for that.

Steve Redgrave: the serious face of a born competitor.

In 1986 Steve was in training for the world rowing championships in Nottingham when a group of friends arrived from Marlow and almost frog-marched him to the nearest municipal golf course. He thought it was an old man's sport and that it held no attraction for him – until the ball started flying. These days, when training permits, he plays in charity events. He won the first he ever entered, a SPARKS day at Wentworth. He was off 24, dense fog held up play but eventually the starter had to let them go. After winning the event with 32 points, Steve confessed that he could do no wrong while the fog was around but once it lifted and he could see where he was supposed to be heading he found the trees with frustrating regularity. Still, as he said in the sunshine of Spain: 'Being able to hit the ball a long way is both a strength and a weakness but I think I've got a nice touch around the green, although my putting has left me at the moment. I don't always hit the ball in the right direction. If I could get that under control I'm sure I could get down to the low teens or even single figures.

'I suppose I play for relaxation. Golf does not relate to rowing at all except that I'm good at one and not very good at the other. It's a change and playing eighteen holes, carrying your own bag which I always do, is quite tiring, especially if you've had two training sessions beforehand. I've played more golf since I've been back from Atlanta than I've ever done in any one period before so I hope to see the rewards of that shortly. I've got to try to accept the frustrations of golf because I know I'm never going to be able to master it. Whatever standard you are, you want to do better. You can be an Olympic gold medallist but you know there's always room for improvement. It's the same with my golf. You go round in ninety and know you can shoot eighty-five. Every round you play you're always going to look back and say you could have done better.'

But I had an overwhelming curiosity about his rowing. I had seen
Steve Redgrave on television, doing his stuff in Los Angeles, Seoul,
Barcelona and Atlanta, and was convinced his cradle must have been
rocked at the Leander Club. Not so.

Steve told me that he had become a rower by accident, though he
was quick to acknowledge the faith and enthusiasm of a schoolmaster
at Great Marlow Comprehensive. 'He was the head of the English
department, a guy called Francis Smith, who had a real love of the
sport. He was not an outstanding rower but he had a feel for it and
enjoyed coaching. He used to go round the boys asking if they wanted
to give it a go and I was one of them. He would look at your hands and
feet because his theory was that if you were big in those departments at
the age of thirteen or fourteen you would grow into a big person who
would be more suited to rowing.'

But rowing came long after he had watched the 1972 Munich
Olympics on television as an eight-year-old and decided that he wanted
to be a champion at the Games, or score the winning goal in the FA
Cup Final, or smash sixes to win the Ashes at Lord's. The rowing
became semi-serious when he was fourteen: 'I got involved with a
coxed four and we went around the domestic circuit. We had seven
races in our first season and won them all. We thought we were God's
gift to rowing. We knew it all and it was going to be so easy. There
were times when it wasn't and there were struggles in the early years,
but long before I became Olympic champion I knew rowing was something I was always going to follow and take to the highest possible
level.

'I'm very much a believer in following fate. A path is set for you but
little things can change it along the way. If I'd made a lot of money from
winning my first gold medal at Los Angeles in 1984 I could have
thought, I've done that, now let's move on to something else, and I
wouldn't have gone on to complete the four. I had a slim chance of getting into the eight that won silver in Moscow in 1980, and if I had it
would have changed the course of my career. I don't think I would have
gone on and reached the heights I've managed since.

'If a lot of money had been involved early on, it would have affected
my direction. But if there had been a lot of money in the last two

Olympics it would not have made any difference. I would have been old enough and mature enough to cope with it while as a teenager it can affect you adversely.'

As we talked I kept thinking of that wonderful moment when he stepped out of the boat with his partner, Martin Pinsent, in the coxless pairs in Atlanta and delivered the immortal line: 'If anyone ever sees me in a boat again, you have my permission to shoot me.' I told him I had a feeling that we would see him rowing at Sydney 2000. He did not deny it. An enigmatic smile flashed across his face and he said: 'There is a possibility that I might row again. I've been able to stay out of it so far but it's quite difficult in some respects. I look at the video of what I said and how I said it and I really did mean it. Now I look back at it and think, that's not true. I think of all the pressure and the way the situation was geared up at the time and the long build-up to it. It was just a relief that we had achieved what we had set out to do and a relief that it was all over. In some respects, if I do carry on, I feel as if I'm going to enjoy it more. I feel that I've been released from the burden of trying to be the first British person to win four consecutive gold medals and I want to go back and I want to enjoy it.'

This took him on to a crusade on behalf of new talented young sportspeople: 'It is important to get the youth geared up to their right sports. The best way to do that is to get the whole nation involved. And the way to do that is to have the Olympic Games in Great Britain. The last two occasions when the Games were in London was almost by default when other countries who were supposed to stage them suddenly couldn't do it. Now I think we should be looking forward to something like 2012 or maybe 2008. We should begin preparing our youth now, as well as gearing up the British public by getting them more interested in the culture of sport because it's becoming very much an industry. We should make that industry more interested in the whole package by trying to put on the best Olympics ever. I think we can do that well. To be honest I don't know where I'm going. I have a big yearning to try to promote new sport. It's very important that the British get back a bit of stature in the world of sport. I just hope we can guide our youth into the sports that are going to suit them.'

It was encouraging to hear a current champion talking so seriously about the future. Redgrave seems to feel that a medal is worth far more than any crock of gold, which is why he wants Britain to do well on the world stage. How had he felt about the generally poor performance in Atlanta?

He has thought about it deeply. 'I felt that we were capable of winning four, five or six gold medals. It just didn't happen. It's very difficult to blame the athletes involved. It's more a structural thing in that we have so few athletes at the top. America has buckets full of athletes with the capabilities to win. If somebody fails they don't get much press because there's always somebody else who will achieve something. We have fewer people at the top and when things don't work out they're the ones who get hounded, and that means more pressure heaped on the individual who has more than he needs anyway. In some respects, rather backhandedly, it may be a good thing that we did so poorly in Atlanta because everybody, from the politicians to the governing bodies, said we can do better. In past Olympics when we came back with five gold medals, the official thinking was that we hadn't done too badly. If we had done that this time they would have said that we were holding our own. But now people are asking what we're going to do about it and there's talk of a National Academy of Sport. It's difficult to say whether or not that will be a benefit. We seem to be playing catch-up all the time. The Australians have had their academy for ten years. Should we be doing something they were doing ten years ago?

'What would the Aussies be doing now if they had their time all over again? We've got to be looking at what is best for us. What is best for the British nation to get better performances in golf, football, cricket, rugby and all the other sports.'

Steve Redgrave is a likeable man. He has been obsessed by establishing himself as a great rower, but when he jumps out of the boat he's as pleasant as the lad next door. He has coped with the fame that arrived without the fortune and when other sportspeople talk in monetary telephone numbers it is reassuring to recognize that his life is centred on the trophy.

The Costa del Sol is the world's golden mile of golf where the rich have their villas, their yachts, and Porto Sotogrande is a living caricature of the good life. Not quite the place, you might think, to find a member of the Russian parliament, one Alexsandr Pavlovich Vladislavlev, standing on the practice ground attempting to hit 7-iron shots into the sunset. I say attempting because, much as I tried to help him with his grip and stance, I felt compelled to deliver my verdict on his progress by borrowing from something I had to say to an old journalist friend, Peter Tory: 'I am the bearer of possibly bad news. Golf may not be the game for you.'

Not surprisingly, Vladislavlev had his own distinctly personal reasons for playing, and all three had a quaint Muscovite logic. He said that, first, age was telling him he was too old for team games; second, that the most important game a man can win is against himself; and third, 'After golf, the meeting with the golf widow is much more attractive than just with the grandmother.' Work that one out for yourself.

Sitting among the yachts, with a whiff of capitalist decadence on the wind, it was incongruous to hear him talk about being taken to the May Day parades in Red Square and then becoming part of the great reforms under Gorbachev and Yeltsin.

In his time Vladislavlev was an outstanding ice hockey player and as such had the opportunity to see what life was like outside the Soviet Union. He confessed that he had had to suppress the desire for liberation that had grown in his mind and which he could not speak about.

Then along came Gorbachev. 'When I heard his first speeches I said to myself that I would follow this man everywhere because he was talking about my dream,' said Vladislavlev. 'It was revenge for a senseless fifty years. But Gorbachev is a contradictory man. First of all, nobody can say a bad word about him because he opened the door. But I do not agree with him on how he did it. When I think of what happened I am reminded about the desert story of the Bedouins who find the bottle with the genie and so on. Gorbachev opened five bottles and everything fell down on the shoulders, minds and brains of people who were not ready for all those changes at once. It's right that the Russians should be awoken but this is not the time to analyse what happened. We will see how it has all worked out in fifty years.

'However, the people are realizing themselves now. They are finding out about private ownership, inflation, financial stabilization, the sovereignty of the republics and so on. They can smell money and believe this is the guarantee of stability. They will never give it back but there are many poor people in conditions which are terribly difficult. There are beggars, people asking for money, the old lady selling a packet of cigarettes. It is a great phenomenon. But the Russians are talented people and they have enormous patience. Patience is the fate of Russia. It is an instrument and it will make all the processes irreversible.'

OVERLEAF Just a hint of the beauty of the old Spain.

97

Alexsandr Pavlovich Vladislavlev: a Russian tries out the capitalist game.

What about Boris Yeltsin?

'I was not among those who supported him at the beginning,' Vladislavlev said. 'When I was first in Russian politics I was in opposition to him but I now understand in this difficult transitional period that he is probably the best. He received the country after Gorbachev, when those genies were still acting, creating movements, consolidating people. Time makes it difficult but he is a man of positive tendencies. He will survive, despite his illnesses, because he is genetically a strong man. I know him from his sporting activities. He was a professional volleyball player.

'Mr Churchill once said that democracy was the worst thing in the world but nobody invented better. His words are not only for Britain but for Russia, who never knew a democracy, especially.'

Vladislavlev had an entertainingly convoluted sense of humour, but he struck me as a man you could trust. He saved me a smile when I said that if he ever became president of Russia I might buy a bijou residence somewhere outside St Petersburg. I suspect he thought I didn't mean it.

One man I would not be anxious to change places with although I admired him greatly was young Martin Pareja Obregon, the matador. For two hours we drove north of Seville, deep into the countryside where the fighting bulls are bred, as much a part of the Spanish culture as flamenco dancers. The car turned off the main road, through a gate and over a cattle grid and we drove for miles through acres of paddocks, scrub, cork oaks and browsing cattle until we came upon a classic Spanish house with a private bullring. I could hear the cry, 'Hey, toro, come on, let's go,' in Spanish as I climbed the few steps to my place of safety behind the barrier.

Martin was training for Sunday's big bull-fight festival in the ancient ring in Seville. It was a stunning experience to see him with his cape, in his suit of lights and, aided by members of his team, playing two bulls. Both were huge black ferocious beasts in their prime. One was a four-year-old, the other six. The tips of their horns had been blunted, presumably because there was no on-site hospital here as there is at the big city corridas.

He allowed a student bull-fighter to play the animals for a while before he went into his own routine of passes, bringing his red muleta over the bull's head so that the beast almost shaved his thighs. Both were strong animals and only the slightest physical flaws – indistinguishable to any-one other than a vet – had prevented them going on to face a matador on the big day in Seville. They were brave, too. After the picador had tested their appetite for a fight they kept coming back for more, twice lifting the heavily padded horse over and onto his side. As an Englishman I viewed it with intense misgivings: there seemed no way that this sport could be justified. But Spain's culture belongs to the Spanish.

After some smart work with the capes and the swords both bulls were killed. It was not a pretty sight and I was reminded of the words of the doyen of all golf writers and commentators, Henry Longhurst, after he had been taken deer-stalking by Lord Castlerosse. Henry shot his stag but later said: 'Well, I've been there. I've seen it and I've done it. But I won't do it again.'

After the bulls had been skinned, quartered and hung in a meat wagon for transportation to the local butchers' shops, we went with Martin to his home. It was a friendly, lived-in place in the country with chicken, dogs and cattle wandering about. There was wine for those who fancied it, and later we sat on a couple of bales of hay in the afternoon sun. I wanted to know about bull-fighting from a matador. I was entranced by the way he talked of his relationship with the animals he slaughtered.

He said: 'The animals are my life. The matador is connected to the animal for many reasons and the bull does not have a corner of my heart, but most of it. It is the animal that gives me life, that loves me and is my companion.

'It is very important to have genes in your blood and for them to be ancestral. My grandfather was a matador and so was my father. Of course, the matador experiences fear before entering the ring but once he is in there he forgets about it. I have been injured two or three times. I have been tossed and struck but there was only one bad injury. The matador does not fight bulls for money. The money is an important part of the career, but the matador is in front of the bull because he is dedi-cated and because he carries the bull's world inside his heart. So he risks his life. I risk my life for my profession because I love it and because it gives me important personal satisfaction which I cannot get from money.

'The bull is my companion,' said Martin Pareja Obregon before going out to kill two.

'I have been a matador for six years. I started when I was very young because my body was telling me so and my life was demanding it. I left everything else behind for the love of bull-fighting. The time to finish is when you start to realize that you no longer have the faculties to be in front of the bull, when you cannot offer the public a spectacle of a certain standard.

'If I was born a thousand times I would always be a matador because the bull, as much as it gives you it takes from you. It gives you a great deal of happiness and a great deal of sadness. But that whole aspect makes my profession beautiful.

'The truth is, though, I would not want my son to follow me into the bull-ring. I would try to guide him in a different direction. But if I could clearly see that he wants to be a matador, that he has the same dedication and passion for it as I do, and that he really wanted to give his life and everything else for bull-fighting, I would not advise him against it. I strongly believe that bull-fighting will never cease to exist. There are many more important things to be ended, like wars and drugs.

'When the matador puts on his suit of lights or starts to look at it laid out on the chair he transforms himself into a matador. It is during those moments when you are dressing yourself that you begin to acquire a certain degree of concentration and to wonder what might happen. You have to make yourself believe that everything is going to go in the best possible way because you will be risking your life, and that is one of the most significant things to consider.

'I train here in the countryside. Nature is one of the most beautiful things because it relaxes you. It allows you to concentrate, to think about the bull-fight. It is very important to condition yourself mentally so that you can face the bull with maximum concentration. I kill some bulls here in the countryside to warm myself up and to be a hundred per cent right physically and mentally.

'For practice I buy bulls from certain livestock breeders. Part of the training is also practising with cows. They are tested to see if they are any good and are then left to breed.'

The pair he had killed had been Bravo bulls, sent to him from a renowned breeder. They had been sent for nothing but, by tradition, Martin sent the money he had received from the butchers to the

Death in the afternoon as bravery is put to the sword in a 'training session'.

breeder. The whole day had been an enthralling experience. But, as Henry had said, once was sufficient.

I was intrigued by Martin's presence. In the ring, even in practice, his movements and command were aloof, strutting, posing with the arrogance demanded of the matador in his suit of lights. Out of the bull-ring he was just another young man in blue jeans and denim shirt looking, perhaps, like an off-duty footballer.

It was in remarkable contrast to our next visit. If you want golf au naturel I recommend the Rio Tinto Club. Here, north-west of Seville, is a gem of enthusiasm where the members are creating their own golf club on reclaimed land at the old Rio Tinto copper mines. The 'fairways' on the little nine-holer are of slate, flint and other stones. Until recently they putted on 'browns', heavily rolled sand that had been oiled around the hole. They still take a piece of matting out with them for 'fairway' shots but now they have built nine proper greens and are working to improve the tees, as well as expanding the little wooden clubhouse that, at a distance, could have passed for a chicken shed but is in fact a cosy centre.

A youngster's enthusiasm is a joy to see at Rio Tinto.

The story of Rio Tinto Golf Club is heart-warming. It is not a case of a huge, multi-national company forking out the pesetas to keep the locals happy. The mine is now almost exhausted and is kept going by workers who took part in a management buy out. They get their water from the mine but little else. They told me that they have four or five away matches each summer because from time to time they obviously love to play on grass and they always win their home matches. It was good to see many children playing golf, and to hear about all the social activities the members were trying to promote.

One of the great enthusiasts was Charles Rich, who was keen to say that golf in these parts had started when British mining engineers began to make their way to Spain in the eighteenth century. He had been born in the area, with an English father and a Spanish mother. The Phoenicians,

105

Left Not a perfect green, but they love it.

apparently, had been the first to realize that the land was hoarding treasure. 'But the people who mined seriously,' said Rich, 'were the Romans who were at it from about 200 BC to AD 300 . Mining stopped for a while and then took up in the modern era with the arrival of the British. They brought their sports with them and, to the astonishment of the local people, there was tennis, polo, football and golf. We believe that just before the end of the last century a golf club was started on the other side of the mine and was called North Lode Golf Club. There is documentation that goes back to 1912 when some of the members asked the general manager of the mine if they could have someone to help with work on the greens.

'That golf course kept going into the sixties, but towards the latter part of the seventies, I understand, it became a part of the working mine and had to be stripped out. At that point golf in the area stopped. Those who were really keen to play migrated to the port of Huelva. Where we are sitting right now used to be a dump,' he said, as we relaxed on an old wooden bench looking up the broken slate road of the first 'fairway'. The few enthusiasts who had wanted to make a golf

Steve Redgrave and his Olympic gold medals with Sebastian Sarria, president of La Cañada Golf Club.

course had restored some kind of shape, planted some hardy trees, and the general manager of the working mine and an old chap from Huelva had come up with a design for five holes.

'A lot of people like myself began to play a particular kind of golf where there was no grass,' he said, and went on to talk about this development close to the site where golf was supposed to have started in Spain, at North Lode. 'The greens were made of compacted sand and the clayish material around the hole we mixed with engine oil. We grew pretty quickly to around forty-five members with probably about sixty licences under the Andalusian Federation. We played throughout the winter until the month of June but shut down between June and September because of the heat when the greens became too hard.

'We have now grown to eighty-two members and a hundred and thirty-five licences. We have also managed to obtain a subsidy from a metallurgical group to enable us to grass the greens. We still have the mats for hitting the ball off the fairway but we now have grass on the greens where, hopefully, the ball will stop and we can play throughout the whole year. We have all the normal hazards and we have "green pegs", which means that if you're not on the fairway you can't use your mat.

'We don't want to stop where we are now, although golf for us is very much a social venture. Whenever we have a tournament there's always lunch and everybody chips in. The kids enjoy it but the club has to progress. We hope to get forty or fifty new members as the news spreads and the course improves. It's a small course. One par five, three par fours and the rest par threes. To grass the whole course from where your first shot lands would not cost all that much and now we have to

OVERLEAF A glimpse of the grandeur of a historic city, Seville.

It's the only way to see old Seville.

look at that possibility. First we would have to put a water supply throughout the whole course. We have a clubhouse, which was paid for by the members. It began as a Portakabin and we built onto it with brickwork. Soon we will be building some proper locker rooms.

'A lot of our members did caddying as youngsters at North Lode Golf Club so golf is nothing new to them. We've got sixteen or seventeen below the age of fourteen. We normally run a tournament once a month and soon, as each project is achieved, we hope to be able to start a golfing school. If we can bring in some kind of a teacher with the help of the Spanish federation it may attract more kids, hence probably more members. We all love to go off and play somewhere else. We always win when the opposition comes here because it can be difficult for someone who has been used to the real thing. Having the ball on the mat helps but the bounce can do all sorts of things.

'As we progress I think we're doing everything right. Each green had its trench dug out by technicians and there's no problem with water, just the logistics of it. We're lucky that the company operating the mine has a fresh water supply that comes straight from the dam and they use it in the mineral process. The water isn't cleansed so we're not tapping into the public's supply. Above the ninth hole we have drilled an Artesian well that has gone down eighty-two metres and allows us to fill a 25,000 litre tank twice a day.'

As we set off to return to Seville I couldn't help smiling at the keenness, and the quality of the swings, of most of the children there. Here was a club that was doing something, really having a go at providing a facility against all the odds and with little funding. They may never be a big fashionable club but there was a camaraderie and spirit about the place that you could only admire.

Somehow they have managed to stretch the course to an 18-hole par of 66 but that is a mere statistic. They have created a unique golf club atmosphere and I couldn't help reflecting, as mothers chatted around a table at the front of the clubhouse and the children went swinging along, that simple pleasures are often the best.

Rio Tinto was a fitting conclusion to the Spanish odyssey and in direct contrast to where we had started, with Jaime Ortiz Patino at Valderrama. Travelling along the road back to Gibraltar airport, and

squeezing out of Spain through the narrow customs post, to a small and
rocky corner of the old Empire, I marvelled at all we had seen.

ALOHA . . . AND FORE!

As you sweep down towards Honolulu airport in your jet aircraft, the Pacific waters around the Hawaiian archipelago grow ultramarine and each island is girdled with surf and sand. The spirit of Aloha, they say, reaches up then to capture your heart but just in case it hasn't within minutes of landing you are welcomed by a girl who places a garland of flowers, known as a *lei*, around your neck with a peck on the cheek.

A glimpse of Pearl Harbor during the aircraft's descent is a reminder that these islands haven't always been tranquil, however, and today Waikiki has skyscrapers and traffic jams. If you're heading north to Turtle Bay and its Hilton Hotel there are freeways to be negotiated. The Polynesian Paradise experience comes later.

This journey to Hawaii was a long one: eleven hours from London Heathrow to San Francisco, a brief wait, then five hours to Honolulu, followed by the ninety-minute drive to the hotel. On arrival, I felt ready for bed but, with a ten-hour time difference, it was only 6 p.m.

The great Hawaiian odyssey was to begin the next day. After four days we were due to leave this island of Oahu for privately owned Lanai, pay a brief visit to the volcanic 'Big Island' of Hawaii and end our golfing journey at Maui. We were to meet the Governor of Hawaii, Benjamin Cayetano, who would see us on the links at Kuilima on the North Shore, Alice Cooper, the original wild man of rock 'n' roll, and the band Hootie and the Blowfish, who had rushed to the top of the American charts. And there would be pineapple plantations, exotic

The spectacle of 14th at the Bay Course, Kapalua.

Governor Benjamin
Cayetano wonders
about his handicap.

wild life, dolphins and whales, the grandest of golf courses and the most luxurious hotels to put a five-star stamp on most of the experiences Hawaii could offer.

Yet there remains something confusing about these lovely islands: even the seasoned traveller tends to believe that Honolulu and Hawaii are the same place when in fact it takes half an hour in a jet to get from one to the other; and while in some respects all the islands seem the same, they are also quite different from each other.

One thing, though, is constant: high-powered golf at high-powered prices has become a major industry. Everything is done to encourage you to spend money: you take a golf cart and you buy something carrying the club's logo. It is difficult to find anywhere with a green fee under $100. The Pearl Golf Club, high on a slope overlooking Pearl Harbor, was an exception at $50 but can only be described as a privately owned, money-making machine at which you queue up, pay your money and play your game, rather like at some of the municipal courses around London at Richmond, Beckenham, and Hainault Forest.

The development of the holiday trade from Japan is intriguing: the runway at Hawaii has just been lengthened to take Jumbo jets and one arrives each week from Tokyo, carrying around 350 golfers who land half an hour away from golf courses at which everything is designed to bring in $500 from every fourball with one every eight minutes.

Before I met the Governor, it seemed appropriate to visit Pearl Harbor. On 7 December 1941, 130 vessels of the US fleet were lying at anchor. Seven battleships were tied up along Battleship Row, among them USS *Arizona*.

At 6.40 a.m. the crew of the destroyer USS *Ward* spotted the conning tower of a midget submarine, heading for the entrance of the harbour, and sank it. Before 7 a.m. the radar station at Opana Point picked up a signal indicating a large flight of planes approaching from the north. They were interpreted as Americans, either from the aircraft carrier *Enterprise* or an expected flight of B-17s from the mainland. No action was taken. The first Japanese aircraft arrived over their Pearl Harbor target areas just before 7.55 a.m. and wave after wave of dive bombers dropped their deadly cargo. More than 2000 personnel were killed. These days, the *Arizona*, the centrepiece of the memorial to the fallen, lies just below the surface of the water in the bay.

We drove back to Turtle Bay through the Dole pineapple plantation and on to our meeting with Governor Cayetano at the Links at Kuilima, next door to our hotel. It is a delightful course, memorable for more than its excellent Arnold Palmer design. For much of the time you play around a huge bird sanctuary, with red cardinals, zebra quail and egrets. It was hard to concentrate on the 17th hole, which was crucial to our match. The Governor is new to golf – he began playing only after he had taken up office. Although he had two bodyguards with him, he was determined to enjoy our day. The 17th is a par four of 452 yards with a string of bunkers about 100 yards from the green, which has the Pacific as a backdrop. Making that distance with a 9-iron third shot proved difficult for the Governor as he had a tendency to 'push' the shot towards the inviting trouble of bunkers and rough beyond.

Our chat took place in a little inlet on the beach, as the surf crashed in and the sun began to set spectacularly. Hawaii became the 50th state of the USA in 1959, making it the youngest. It had its own monarchy until 1893 and I was interested to know what had gone wrong.

The Governor explained: 'The Queen wanted to restore some rights she felt had been lost to the Hawaiian people by the legislature of those days which was dominated by wealthy plantation owners and the like. There was a kind of constitutional monarchy but then the American sugar planters got wind of her intentions to restore the full monarchy so they amassed a militia and, with bayonets on their rifles, they forced the signing of what was known as the Bayonet Constitution and the Queen was overthrown. She spent the rest of her life in the mansion where I live now, Washington Place. After Hawaii was annexed by the United States in 1898 she refused to fly the American flag until news reached her in 1917 that some Hawaiian citizens had died in World War I in the service of the United States. Then she is reported to have said, "If my people love this nation so much there should be some reconciliation." Next morning she hoisted the American flag. It's a very touching story.

117

Just a word at twilight with the Governor.

But the Hawaiian flag features a little Union Jack in one corner. What is its significance?

'Well Captain Cook discovered Hawaii for the western world and there are many places here where the British presence is still noticeable. You can see it in the historical remnants and some of the ceremonies that we celebrate. Look at the Royal Guard. The uniform is very much like that of certain British troops.

'We have a palace that is clearly influenced by Europe because many of our monarchs were trained and educated abroad and could speak three or four languages. We are heavily steeped in and influenced by European monarchy.'

Once you switch off from the dollar-churning golf industry and take time to look at the islanders, you discover their unique friendliness and courtesy. Governor Cayetano is clearly a man of his people. He was born in Hawaii of Filipino immigrant parents who had little money but plenty of energy. He told me how a former governor, an Irishman called Jack Burns, recruited him to politics after he had returned from the

'I think it falls from
the left, sir.'

119

mainland having qualified as a lawyer. The Aloha spirit, he said, had a lot to do with his involvement. The young Benjamin Cayetano was a Democrat and a keen supporter of President John F. Kennedy but had not thought of politics as a career for himself. However, when he had been about to embark on his early cases he found himself appointed to an important commission by Governor Burns.

As Mr Cayetano puts it: 'I had never met Jack Burns in my life. When I finally did I thanked him for appointing me and asked him why he had. He looked at me and said: "There are not many Filipinos who go to college and become attorneys." His idea was to reach out and bring together the different segments of the population. That is why he is still well thought of today and part of that is a product of the Aloha spirit, which is hard to define but, to me, it is the glue that holds this community together. Quite frankly, I would consider that if it could be transported to other places it would be Hawaii's gift to the rest of the world. The Aloha spirit is at the core of Hawaiian culture. It is basically to be caring and tolerant. All of the ethnic groups here have grown up virtually side by side. As for religions, you name 'em, we got 'em all.

'I would say we are happier than most American states. We probably have the highest incidence of interracial marriages. The one anxiety I have, maybe more than crime or anything else, concerns the young people of this state, and it probably applies all over the country. I wonder if they are losing touch with their history, maybe their roots and their culture. It is really important for all the different groups in this state not only to work together but to do the things that will teach the young culture and history.'

Mr Cayetano is clearly proud of the improvements in general education that have been made in Hawaii, but saddened by the decline of the sugarcane and pineapple industries: some Caribbean and Asian governments subsidize their own growers and can undercut Hawaiian prices. This may explain the surge in golf as a

120

The Governor is quite nifty with his 9-iron.

major tourist business. These days, the Japanese are welcome visitors to the islands, but I wondered if the welcome they receive is in close relation to the amount of money they spend. The Governor said: 'President Clinton was here when we celebrated the fiftieth anniversary of Pearl Harbor and I recall a ceremony in my office, meeting with three US veterans of the raid and three Japanese pilots. These men were all in their seventies. It was one of the most touching things I have ever seen because the interchange indicated that this was a time for reconciliation, a time to shake hands and go forward, and I really think that is how the people of this state feel. I do not know anyone who harbours any resentment towards the Japanese for what happened fifty years ago.'

OVERLEAF A stunning view of the 8th at Koele.

121

Lanai is a rich man's paradise, where luxury is alive and well. It used to be called Pineapple Island but now the crop raised is minimal and the 2800 inhabitants, most of whom live in single-storey wood-framed cottages, tend to work in tourism, which centres around two sumptuous hotels, the Lodge at Koele and the Manele Bay Hotel, and their golf courses.

We were a couple of weeks too early to see the Humpback whales that make their way from Alaska to the straits between Lanai and Maui to calve and mate before heading back to the colder Alaskan waters. During the autumn and spring season, the whales cavort with the Hawaiian spinner dolphins. I was told a story of how, when a female whale was giving birth, sharks began to move in, sensing an easy meal, but the dolphins formed a protective circle around her and repelled the marauders.

The bay has wonderfully clear shark-free water with coral reefs that make snorkelling a rewarding pastime while inland you can enjoy the glorious scenery, horse trails, hiking and, of course, golf.

Alice Cooper wanted to play at the Experience at Koele, a par 72 that is 2300 feet above sea level, designed by Greg Norman with Ted Robinson as architect. He also wanted to play the Challenge at Manele Bay, which runs along the water and is a par 72 Jack Nicklaus creation that can truly claim to offer a view of the ocean at every hole. Alice Cooper's stage act was designed to make outrage funny and he adopted the name 'to irritate every parent in America'. From this you may get a hint of what was to come in our meeting.

When we met at the Experience course, set high among eucalyptus, Norfolk and Cook Island pine groves, with wild turkey and francolin fowl strutting about, Alice looked a bit like a peacock himself. Blue shirt, white trousers and his black hair pulled back into a pony-tail under a golfing visor, he seemed ready for the waterfalls, dog legs and undulations of a course of tiers, gorges and tradewinds. And some very shy Axis deer.

The classic golfing double at Lanai is to play the Experience early in the morning, when there may be a sweater's worth of chill in the air, take a snack, and then move down to the Challenge, into the shorts and away, completing your thirty-six holes in time to watch the sunset from the veranda with a cold beer or, perhaps, a Mai Tai – a dark and white rum speciality of the islands that has a knack of creeping up on you. Many a golfer, I suspect, may have gone a glass too far.

Not Alice Cooper, though. He hasn't had a drink for fifteen years. Now his addiction is to golf. He is a round-a-day man with a handicap of five, whose public image seems far removed from reality. According to a recent press release, 'Alice Cooper has never disappointed. Throwing cash back into the uplifted faces of those who made him rich, ripping the heads off baby dolls, dancing with the dead and depicting his own demise and resurrection. Alice Cooper on stage has had himself beheaded, electrocuted, beaten up by a gang of thugs, fought with monsters and mad dentists, escaped from straitjackets and black widows. No one leaves an Alice Cooper show feeling calm.'

I thought of those words as we stood on the eighth tee at the Experience, described in the brochure as: 'The signature hole, this 390 par four presents a 200 foot drop in elevation from tee to green. The hole is nestled in the deepest and most magnificent gorge on the island. It is sure to become one of the most spectacular and talked about golf holes in the world. The green is guarded to the right by a 70 foot sentinel eucalyptus, so be warned to play your drive to the left. Trade winds usually blow from the right.'

We played from the 417 yards tee (440 yards being the championship mark). The elevation is interesting, the fairway below is generously wide but any shot drifting to the right is likely to be caught up in the decorative water hazard with its little tumbling waterfall, hibiscus flowers and

African tulip trees. In some aspects it was like a longer version of the 17th hole at Castle Combe in Wiltshire, which Clive Clark and I did a few years ago. You've got to get from high ground to low ground, then down the hill on a zigzag path. The 17th at Castle Combe is only 160 yards from the back tees. This one at Koele is dramatic, interesting and it looks very natural but is, in fact, artificial: as you look into the ravine you can see the little rockery, the waterfall and the cart path on the left. The 'signature hole' is a new phrase that has crept into usage, and supposedly denotes a hole that carries the architect's stamp. I have done 80 or 90 courses and people have asked me how I left my signature. I tell them I haven't – yet. All this signature talk came about because Pete Dye used railway sleepers, like the old Prestwick bunkers, in his early course design. To be honest I thought the eighth at the Experience just slows the game with people getting their cameras out and waiting until the light is right before they take a shot.

Alice Cooper reflects on a solid round.

Well, Alice hit a purler 250 yards down the middle past the trap and was not far behind me. His 8-iron floated in gently and my 9-iron was alongside. Halved in four seemed a reasonable outcome. We had a splendid day and came to the conclusion that if I went on a diet and he could stop hitting the ball occasionally to the right, we might form a formidable fourball or foursomes partnership in pro-am competitions.

Alice Cooper once allegedly bit the head off a chicken on stage. He also had a number of hits in the seventies with songs like 'School's Out' and 'No More Mr Nice Guy'. His trademark outrageous make-up and suggestive stage act created such a storm of disapproval that Mary Whitehouse and Leo Abse MP, those great British reformers and arbiters of taste, had him banned from the United Kingdom.

After our round we sat in the gardens of the Lodge by the carp pond surrounded by exotic shrubs. In this peaceful stetting Alice emerged. He is bright, articulate, forthright, religious, self-deprecating and frequently referred to his alter ego Alice Cooper in the third person. He said: 'When I do a concert now my audience's ages range from thirteen to fifty. The kids

who were going to our shows in the seventies now have teenage kids and they say, "You wanna see rock 'n' roll, come on I'll show you rock 'n' roll, come and see Alice, he started it all." It's funny to see the variance in age.

'Alice is a character I created pretty much to hide behind. I'm not much of a show-off at all but Alice is. When I play Alice I play the character the way Jack Nicholson would play the Joker. I try to make the character as opposite to myself as possible so that I have fun playing him. He is much more Captain Hook, the kind of villain you actually like. Alice just came from a long history of reading comic books, watching horror movies and all the Americanisms rolled into a modern day Frankenstein. Alice is a media monster. He takes a little bit from here and a little bit from there and when you see him he is America gone crazy.

'We tried to come up with a name that was going to irritate every parent in America. Here's these five guys with long hair and tattoos and all this stuff. What are we going to call them? Let's call them something really nice.

'Alice Cooper was the sweetest name we could think of and it just bothered everybody, especially when they realized that nobody in the band was gay. We were like a study in opposites. Nobody was into drugs. We drank beer and watched football. Everybody in the band was a four-year letterman in high school. We were all athletes. We played the Alice Cooper image to the hilt. Any time anybody came up with a rumour about Alice our main thing was never to deny it. You don't want to ruin the ambience about Alice Cooper. We threw it in everybody's face. The Americans didn't get it at first, but the British did.

'When Mary Whitehouse and Leo Abse banned us, that was the best thing that could have happened. It helped our cause. Any time you get banned in Britain you're doing great. The record went immediately to number one and that was without our taking a step on British soil. It was just a matter of rumour and a tidal wave of publicity. At that point you don't have to do anything. You just let the audience's imagination go crazy. We did what was literally a Broadway show. *Welcome to My Nightmare* was a Broadway show based on horror and comedy, a pre-*Rocky Horror Picture Show*. Away from all that we were absolutely courteous. We were the most professional band out there. What looked like all this horror on stage was very rehearsed. We spent months and

A par four here is a prize indeed - the 8th at Koele.

127

months in rehearsal and all the money we made on tour went back into the show to make it even bigger and better. We were never late.

'We probably rehearsed three times more than any other band, because if you're going to put your head in a guillotine and it's got to look like your head is coming off, it better be really good. That blade only missed me by six inches every night and it was a forty-pound blade. But those stories about tearing animals apart and so on just didn't happen.

'Take the great story about the chicken for one thing. We were doing a show in Toronto, the first time anybody in Canada had ever seen Alice Cooper. It was being filmed, there were sixty thousand people in the place and John Lennon and Jim Morrison were among them. At the end of the show we would take feather pillows and open them up and with two cartridges we had hidden we made it look like a blizzard on stage, and this with all the noise going on. Somebody from the audience threw a chicken on stage. Now I have never been on a farm in my life. I am from Detroit but I know that a chicken has feathers and wings and can fly. I picked it up and it was fine so I just threw it back and assumed it would fly away. It landed in the audience and they tore it to pieces and threw the parts back on stage. The next day it was in the paper, "Alice Cooper Rips Head Off Chicken and Drinks the Blood." It was full of all this stuff . . . I went, "Wow, I didn't see that." Frank Zappa, who was our producer at the time, called me and asked me if I'd ripped the head off the chicken. When I said no, he said, "Well don't tell anyone. We love it."

'At the time it was all happening so fast, but the topper on that was that the first eight rows were all wheelchairs so they were the people who tore the chicken apart. That made it even more bizarre because they were more vicious than anyone else. Maybe they just wanted the chicken as a souvenir.'

Alice appears to have been lucky with his management advisers and with his wife Sheryl, a former ballerina, who has been married to him for twenty years. He said: 'I have had the same manager for twenty-eight years. I was one of the lucky guys in that my manager was my best friend, Shep Gordon. We never had a contract together and still don't. Our credo was simple: if I have money, you have money, and if you have money, I have money. Our relationship started off as a total lie. It was the only time we have ever lied to each other. I told him I was a singer and he told me he was a manager and that was how we started. We ended up having to make ourselves good.

'I never went into any bizarre money-making schemes. I always said pay your taxes and do what you're supposed to do. The only way you can get into trouble is by not doing that. We always invested in safe things. My first cheque was for a hundred thousand dollars when I was twenty-one. That was so much money it was ridiculous. Shep wouldn't let me spend a penny of it. He made me buy a house. He said if everything else failed I would at least have a house. I was going to buy eight Ferraris but I reckoned a house would be all right.

'I still have the house in Paradise Valley and it's worth ten times what I paid for it. He was smart enough to see that coming.'

He spoke frankly about his alcohol addiction: 'There was a period when I just couldn't perform or travel because I was an alcoholic. I was drinking a bottle of whisky a day. I'd get up in the morning and throw up blood. I wouldn't tell anybody about it because I wasn't eating. I was just drinking and surviving. But I was never drunk. I could walk a straight line. I never slurred a word. I never missed a show and nobody knew I had a real drinking problem until it was too late. I checked into a hospital and it's fifteen years now since I had a drink. I'm forty-eight and I always tell people that I am in better shape now than I was twenty years ago and that's the real truth. I had my bouts. I knew Jim Morrison, Keith Moon, Jimi Hendrix, and I saw them all go down. These guys were friends and I knew how fast they were living. I just figured that they were going to play life for what it was and nobody wanted to grow old.'

Alice went on to talk about the power of his wife's influence on him and he told me that his father and father-in-law were pastors. He has three children: a daughter Calico, then fifteen, an eleven-year-old son, Dash, and three-year-old Sonora. They all live happily together in Arizona. He met Sheryl some time after she had auditioned for a role in his stage show: 'She was a classically trained ballet dancer who had no idea who Alice Cooper was. I didn't want rock 'n' roll dancers in the show. I wanted her for a song called 'Only Women Bleed', which was a big hit at the time. It was going to be a ballet and I said I wanted a real ballerina. She tried out with seventeen hundred other girls and got the

129

OPPOSITE No headless chickens this time for Alice Cooper.

part. I didn't pick her. I didn't even notice her until half-way through the tour because we were so busy. Then I saw her and we fell in love and got married. She had a lot of faith. She just figured that one day I would straighten out and she would be the influence on me and it was true.

'Dash was ten when he had a hole-in-one – 154 yards with a Big Bertha driver. He asked me if he had to buy drinks for everyone. He's got a great business going. I told him I'd give him twenty-five cents for every good ball he brought home and in ten days he brought me a thousand. Then I said he had to learn about supply and demand. I didn't need any more golf balls therefore it would in future be ten cents per ball. He brought home another eight hundred so I had eighteen hundred golf balls in a matter of weeks.'

Whatever happened to that putting touch.

It looks like team uniforms at Koele.

The eyes that are plastered with maniacal make-up whenever he is gyrating on stage brightened at the talk of golf. It was as though he had been waiting for the invitation to indulge in his golfing fantasies. He even sees a future on the fairways. 'I play so much golf I want to get into the golf business somehow,' he said. 'I don't know how or where or why. I'm not good enough to play the Senior Tour but I might take two years off and practise hard just to see the looks on some of the faces when they see the hair. All I want to do is shoot par. I don't want to win a tournament. I just want to play with these guys.

'Golf was a big part of my rehabilitation. I'm an addictive person. I get really hooked. That's why I can't drink. I was addicted to alcohol and I loved it. I loved the taste of beer and I loved the taste of whisky until I got to be such an alcoholic that I couldn't stand the taste. That's when I knew I was in trouble, when I hated the taste and was still drinking it. It was like feeling good for no real reason. You should do something to feel good so when I stopped drinking I started playing thirty-six holes a day. I just went out and started hitting some balls because I knew that if I sat in my house I would begin thinking about drinking. I immediately became addicted to golf. The better you play in this game the more addicted you become. Instead of hitting two or three good shots one day I hit seven or eight. Then maybe nine or ten and pretty soon I was hitting sixty or sixty-five good ones in a round.

'In the last ten years golf has become cool and Tiger Woods is the most important thing in the game right now because he is going to influence a lot of kids who would normally be in trouble. When they are looking to get out of the ghetto or the inner city they may be thinking they have the choice of picking up a Uzi or a 3-iron. It may occur to them that they can get into a lot less trouble selecting the golf club. Tiger Woods is giving them the chance to do that. He's a really good role model.

'I love the game. I love it when I come out and see an eighty-nine-year-old guy hitting the ball down the middle. It makes me think I might have another thirty or forty years of playing. For years I didn't keep a handicap because I just liked to go out and hit the ball. I played every day but usually with an assistant pro or the pro himself and it was like taking a daily golf lesson. Your handicap is going to come down. I probably went from thirty to six in two years. I was down to two and realized that you have to play the game of your life every time you go out.'

The urge to entertain had recently rekindled itself in Alice Cooper. He said: 'I went out last year for the first time in four years and toured fifty-two cities this summer. I had a great time. Great response. Rock 'n' roll has grown up a bit. Vintage bands such as Eagles, Kiss and so on are going out again and now all their old fans are financially fluid. They are drawing fifty thousand people a night which, in many cases, is more than they drew first time round. The same thing is happening with us. We go out and people are buying a little slice of their past. As far as I'm concerned, when I go out to do a show it's with the same professionalism and attitude as when I was eighteen. I've got to be up there as strong as I was then.

'There will always be new things in the show. We're in an interesting situation. If you go to see the Rolling Stones you want to hear the hits.

It's a tough one over the ocean at The Challenge at Manele Bay.

134

It's the same with Alice Cooper. You want to hear 'School's Out' 'Eighteen' and 'No More Mr Nice Guy' – but you also want to *see* the hits. Those classic Alice bits, maybe the magic screen, the straitjacket, and then we'll try to add something more. I'm still making new records and trying to outdo my last one. I have no intention of living in the past. I want to compete with the new bands. I enjoy doing the extravaganza. My idea of great audience reaction was never a huge "Yeah". I wanted more of a whispered, "Wow, what was that?" An audience that was totally dumbfounded was the best reaction.

'My favourite band was always The Yardbirds from England. Queen was very dramatic and precise, and the Beatles were the guys who opened the door. We learned every Beatles song that there ever was and the same with the Stones. My parents hated the Beatles when they first saw them but then they saw the Stones and decided the Beatles were not that bad after all. As soon as I saw the Stones I reckoned I could put

'I think I rather enjoyed that shot'.

together an act that would make them look like kindergarten stuff. I thought that if the Stones could scare my parents I could scare them even worse.

'One thing, though. I never promoted drugs. And there was never anything in our stage act that was anti-Christian. I would never do the Satanic thing. That always offended me since I came from a Christian household. I was always God-fearing. There was never any nudity or swearing. We were purely a side-show. We had a lot of fun with ridiculous violence. I think I related more to *Monty Python* because sometimes they would do some of the most ridiculously violent things and it turned the corner and became funny. I always wanted Alice to have a funny edge. I never wanted to scare people as much as I wanted them to be afraid and then laugh.'

Alice Cooper is a good talker and tells a good story. And that day he played a splendid round over the Challenge at Manele Bay, where he finished just three over par on a course tougher than the average resort course, though his card was aided when he holed out from a greenside bunker for birdie on the par five ninth. He played the golf course with an almost feverish determination to master it. The 12th was lying in wait.

Signature springs to mind on this one, with its 200-yard carry from the back tee over an inlet with the ocean 150 feet below, crashing against the rocks. It reminded me of a world's most difficult holes calendar, in which you need to be a mountaineer, scuba diver, SAS soldier and astronaut all rolled into one. It was difficult and some members of our party who tried to play it were merely donating balls to the ocean – and they knew it before they teed up. Alice hit a 3-wood and just made it. I was reminded of other holes with similarly dramatic backgrounds of cliffs, pounding water and rising spray: at Val de Lobo in the Algarve where Henry Cotton created a green beyond the cliffs, and at Pebble Beach, Cypress Point, Turnberry, and the wonderful courses in the west of Ireland. The 12th hole at the Challenge was a good one from every tee except the 65-yard one. From the back tee it was a 2-iron for me but across the bay the wind obviously knocks the ball down towards the water.

Lanai is owned by the Dole Corporation and the island's hotels are outstanding. The whole ambience at both oozes luxury. The contrast with the golf was interesting. It is all very well to tell people that they should play from the tee that suits their game and from which they will draw most enjoyment but they often seem reluctant to do that. There are five or six tees on each hole at the Experience (Norman) and the Challenge (Nicklaus) but I suspect many of the forward tees are hardly ever used.

Both courses were interesting although not in particularly good condition: at the Challenge it was difficult to keep the grass, due to the prevailing climatic conditions but also because a hundred people play the course every day.

Our brief trip to Hawaii was to look at golf among the volcanic clinker of Mauna Lani, half an hour from Hawaii airport. Driving out towards the course, the landscape consists of mile after mile of black, treeless lava rock until you come to the oasis of the golf course where every tee is booked, it seems, by either Japanese or American tourists. The course is a par 72 of 6913 yards and one of the features is the short 12th, a hole of 132 yards over an enormous, single volcanic rock standing eighteen feet high in the middle of a bunker.

137

Be good! It was, on Hawaii at Mauna Lani.

The unique experience of the Lava at Mauna Lani.

It was a simple enough hole for a good player but we thought it would be fun to try to bounce the ball off the lava rocks that formed a high horse-shoe around the hole. It didn't work. Anything hit up there stayed trapped unless you hit a clean rock on the face pointing towards the green. Perhaps I had offended Moki, a malevolent Hawaiian elf: folklore said that he was hiding in there and if he liked you he threw your ball back onto the fairway.

The lava is like a water hazard – good-bye, ball. Someone once drew an interesting comparison between bunkers and water: a bunker is a road crash, an accident you might easily survive; a water hazard is an aeroplane crash – you've gone and there's no return. In some ways Mauna Lani reminded me of the Aga Khan's course in the top right-hand corner of Sardinia, the Costa Smeralda, which is also hewn from rocks. You go off the fairway and the ball is lost. There are others like this in the desert, around Phoenix and Palm Springs. It is hard to walk on and if you do, you risk breaking an ankle.

Losing golf balls does not seem to cause the same acute pain to Americans and Canadians and other golfers as it does to the British. They want to play these difficult courses for the sake of having played them: American golfers visit the Tournament Players' Championship course at Sawgrass, Florida, to play to the island green at the short 17th even if it means putting eleven balls into the water.

Kapalua is probably the best known of Hawaii's golf centres, and we had a date there with Hootie and the Blowfish, a highly successful American rock 'n' roll band whose first album *Cracked Rear View* sold several million copies and is still high on many best-selling charts around the world. Their second, *Fairweather Johnson*, is threatening now to overtake it.

Kapalua is a shrine to golf on a historical old site. There are now three courses alongside the Ritz-Carlton Hotel, all of outstanding quality and

139

Hootie and the Blowfish discuss strategy on Maui.

difficulty. The scenery is stunning, whether you are on the Bay course (6600 yards, par 72), the Village course (twisting and turning, rising and falling through the West Maui foothills with a par 71, 6632 yards challenge) or the Plantation course (par 73, 7263 yards). Kapalua is committed to preserving wildlife by conserving water, providing food and limiting the use of pesticides. If you ever have the chance to play there, keep an eye open for the spotted doves, frigate birds and black-crowned night herons. The Plantation is the newest course. The showpiece of the three, it was designed by Ben Crenshaw and Bill Coore and opened in 1991. It unfurls across island canyons and panoramic ocean plateaux.

Kapalua has been the venue for USPGA tournament events and the Plantation was being prepared for the Lincoln Mercury International.

While we were filming Hootie and the Blowfish on the 17th green I heard an English voice in the distance calling: 'Get a move on, you plonkers.' Back down the fairway and waiting to come through were the European tour players Darren Clarke and Barry Lane with their caddies on a practice round. As Clarke has a distinctive Ulster brogue, suspicion fell on Lane as the joker!

Hootie and the Blowfish were very respectable golfers. The band is composed of singer Darius Rucker, guitarist Mark Bryan, bassist Dean Felber and drummer Jim 'Soni' Sonefeld, who wore a golf shoe that would have turned a British golf club secretary apoplectic. He favoured open-toed sandals, with a sole thick enough to be adequately spiked, and no socks, with loose, knee-length shorts. It is a uniform that apparently goes down well in the Carolinas from where the band hails. At Muirfield it might not work.

They are all golf nuts, almost as fiendishly addicted to the game as Alice Cooper, and their roadshows are scheduled to allow the maximum time for golf. The maker of the steel crates used to transport their instruments received an additional order for containers to carry golf clubs. Hootie and the Blowfish began to play together at the University of South Carolina when Bryan, who had played with Mark at high school, heard Darius singing along to the radio. Soni soon followed and together they worked the small town circuit on the eastern seaboard of the United States, driving from gig to gig, sleeping between amplifiers and dreaming of the big time, which came with the explosion of *Cracked Rear View.*

Mark and Dean had always been keen on golf. They grew up together in Maryland in a wealthy, middle-class community. Their fathers worked for big corporations and weekends involved family outings to the local country club, where the boys had lessons from the club pro. Darius played golf long before he thought of becoming a singer: his father's best friend played at an airforce base. When Soni joined the band, he realized that if he was to get along with the others, golf was a necessity.

Darius Rucker and 'Soni' Sonefeld, laid-back singers with Hootie and the Blowfish.

There is still a refreshing, college-boy normality about them. They get on well together, speak politely and are criticized sometimes back home for being so average-nice. As Darius said: 'Criticizing us for being normal makes me want to laugh. So we like to play golf, we're friends with the same people we were friends with in college and we live in the same town . . . big deal. We get a lot of crap about playing golf. Who says rock 'n' rollers can't play golf? I've played with Alice Cooper, who's pretty damn good.'

Hootie and the Blowfish can look after themselves on the course, too. I was impressed with the way they played on the morning after one of their entourage's stag-night celebrations. The only sign that anything in their preparation had gone wrong came when Darius coaxed a follower to call the hotel to ask them to prepare eggs Benedict as he would be along the moment he finished the game. That call was made on the 17th at the Plantation, a long, sweeping par five with a deep ravine to be cleared with the second shot from what is invariably a downhill lie. All four negotiated it well. They had good putting strokes, although Soni's putter looked more like a museum piece than the modern equipment favoured by the others, and Dean was in so many bunkers that he had to say: 'Don't worry, sand is my speciality.'

We sat around for a while afterwards – the eggs Benedict had to wait – to talk about the band's success and their attitude to life. Darius spoke first: 'We've been together a long time. We've been a band for eleven

OVERLEAF
Crashing surf is the backdrop to Kapalua Bay Course's 5th hole.

years and everything stays in the family basically. We were teenagers together until we were twenty-five. We're around thirty now and we're still teenagers. It took us nine years to be an overnight success.'

Mark went on: 'People approach it as though we came round yesterday. We were running around the Carolinas, writing our own songs. Everybody chips in and offers music and words. We can all play different instruments. Soni, our drummer, is not afraid to sit down and write a song for guitar or piano. Everybody can play acoustic guitar and everything comes very much from that format. Once we start from there we can take a song anywhere. We all grew up playing sports and as you get older you realize that golf is a game you can play for your entire life. We probably latched on to it because you can bring your clubs on the road and it is a good chance to get away from the bus and the show. It's a chance to get out with nature for four hours and just hit it around.'

Golf's image, however, did not seem to fit easily with that of show business, I suggested, in which people are commonly supposed to stay up until at least two a.m. lie in bed till four in the afternoon then play pool or snooker and finally go to work – apart, of course, from notables like Bing Crosby and Bob Hope who played golf to a high standard.

It was Soni's turn: 'It's a nice change of pace for what we do for a living. It's literally one of the few times in the day when we can be ourselves, out on the golf course breathing fresh air and out of the typical rock 'n' roll scenario. Nobody is ever rude to us but you get people following you all the time asking for autographs. It's hard for any of us to go anywhere without being bothered a little bit but out here you can hide in the middle of the fairway. We've also been lucky enough to surround ourselves with people we trust. We don't have a bad time. We make our decisions together. We've been through the bad times already. The hardest were driving around the Carolinas in a van smelling of these guys' feet. Now it's a lot easier.'

Dean said little. He is clearly the quietest of the four, almost cherubic looking. He could almost have passed as an accountant. Mark carried on: 'The funny thing is that we probably party as much as any of the rock 'n' roll guys but we just don't have a reputation for it. We were brought up as polite kids. Our families taught us to be respectful of people and things and we have never lost that. We can still have a good

144

time without making people angry. We enjoy what we do. We don't take for granted where we are and we all feel we're lucky to be in this situation.'

I was impressed by them: they've got a style, something good happened and off they were. And it was good to hear Mark talk so positively of how they had been brought up.

It was sad to leave Hawaii: the spirit of Aloha had seeped into us. There is a hint of tomorrow-will-do about it but it sits nicely with the ambience of the sun and sea and the timelessness of the volcanic mountains. As our jet headed for the clouds, the cold and damp of a British winter, I thought again of Governor Cayetano. Unlike many top politicians he came across as a caring, genuine person, who gave me the impression that he could get things done.

145

I couldn't help feeling as we left behind the pineapples and golf courses of the Hawaiian islands that they could not be in better custody than that of the man who had just taken up the ancient game of steering a little white ball from tee to cup.

THE LONGEST DAWN

Visiting South Africa was an adventure that began at the Steenberg winery near Cape Town with Sir Garfield Sobers, the legendary West Indian cricketer, and ended at Silver Lakes Golf Club, Pretoria, in the company of F. W. de Klerk, leader of the opposition to Nelson Mandela's African National Congress but an architect of the dismantling of apartheid. I also had a memorable reunion with Gary Player and played golf with Andrew Mlangeni, an MP, aged seventy-one, who had been imprisoned altogether for twenty-six years and four months, most of the time with Mandela on the infamous Robben Island.

Steenberg is one of the oldest estates on the Cape, nestling between the white sands of False Bay and the rear view of Table Mountain. Wine was first produced on these gentle slopes more than three hundred years ago but it was only recently, when a new company took over the estate and created the golf course, that production picked up again. The Cabernet Sauvignon served in the restaurant was a particularly lusty red.

As we drove along the drive, which was lined with oak trees, I was quite taken with the style of the place; its white-painted buildings, the lawns, the regimented lines of vines and the golf course, which although it is very new is commendably mature in its condition. Broken ground indicated that much development was still going on and there are plans to build 220 houses round the edges of the golf course. That a hundred had been sold in a matter of months indicated that the area is much sought-after.

Alongside the tee at Steenberg

Sir Gary Sobers, the face of a legend.

The golf course is an example of the work of Peter Matkovich. It was of an impressive design, moving through six holes of parkland, with tee boxes often elevated above the vineyards, then dropping down to what are called the wetlands, with reed-ringed water courses, before the last few holes across Cape heathland.

I remembered Peter Matkovich from years ago as a young professional arriving in Britain with the Wilkes brothers, Harold Henning and Cobie Le Grange. It was pleasing to see that his world of golf had progressed to architect level.

Steenberg Country Hotel and Golf Estate offers seventeen guest rooms. The accommodation is elegant, furnished with dark wood and cleverly designed to reflect the style of the seventeenth and eighteenth centuries, whose comforts were enhanced for me by the knowledge that my neighbour and playing partner was Sir Garfield Sobers. Millions of words have been written about his play, his conduct, his captaincy skills and his lust for life, and his cricketing record with the West Indies, his native Barbados and his adopted Nottinghamshire is truly astonishing. His Test innings of 365 not out stood for thirty-six years before Brian Lara topped it in 1994, and Gary was there to hug him when he did it at St Johns, Barbados. Gary hit 26 Test centuries, took 235 wickets, held 110 catches and captained West Indies 39 times before he was sacked after a typically bold declaration: in 1968 at Port o' Spain, Trinidad, he set England 215 runs to get in 165 minutes. England achieved the target with three minutes to spare, Colin Cowdrey making 71 and Geoff Boycott still there at 80 not out. I'm told that even today you can still get a good argument going by raising the subject in the Caribbean.

Whenever Gary Sobers played cricket something thrilling happened. He was a player who hustled and bustled, forever experimenting with his spin bowling, and if that didn't work he would try a few medium pacers. He shone with joy whether he was making a catch or stroking good bowling around the field usually finding the gaps with unerring accuracy. He never seemed to be aware of just how good he was, although he could not resist a joke at the expense of his great friend and rival, Fred Trueman. 'Fred used to say that I was his bunny,' he laughed, 'because he got me out when I was 226 and 198. Fred was a great bowler who could show today's men where and how to pitch the ball.'

Gary says simply that he saw himself always as a team man. If they needed runs, he would give it a bit of a swing. He was one of most successful West Indian cricket captains, winning three consecutive tours including one in Australia. He is a delightful companion, and although he is now entering his sixties (he was born in July 1936) with bad knees and a stiff lower back, he delighted me with the elegance and fluency of his golf swing.

The way he swept through the ball with such abandon reminded me of that day in Swansea in 1968 when he struck the Glamorgan bowler Malcolm Nash for six consecutive sixes. He and Nash still meet when they are in the same area and Nash tells Gary that he was trying to dismiss

OVERLEAF Some of the scenery is unsurpassed.

149

The old, familiar cricketer's swing works well.

him with every delivery, working on the theory that he must miss or mis-hit one ball. I felt something similar as he came down the eighteenth at Steenberg, a par five of 483 metres, from a tee tucked away among the trees.

Away to the left were the white post-and-rails of a stud with four yearlings tossing their heads and swishing their tails. In the stream ahead four ducklings tried to keep up with their mother in a pleasant cameo of the Cape spring. Gary's main concern was launching his drive down the middle and that trusted swing, which once got him down to scratch and off a handicap of two for sixteen years, did not let him down. He laid up with a 4-iron and pitched to eighteen inches for a birdie with a stylish aplomb that any senior professional would have relished.

It amused us that he wore a golf glove on both hands where most golfers favour only one, on the top hand on the club. Gary, a left-hander, explained: 'I've always played with two gloves. It comes from the batting gloves. Without wearing two for golf my hands felt weak. My hands are quite soft – in fact, people ask me how I managed to play cricket with hands like these.' Then he remarked that if he could choose his career again it would be in golf. He is in love with the game.

Note the two gloves and the high finish.

After we had played I wanted to see him hit a few balls on the driving range. He was truly immaculate, and although, of course, it is impossible to say how far he might have gone as a professional golfer, it was clear that his gifts are natural and rich.

Gary Sobers has always been a modest man, but he was genuinely overwhelmed when he realized that his knighthood had been the idea of former British Prime Minister Sir Harold Wilson rather than at the nomination of the Barbados government. As we sat on the Steenberg lawn sipping orange juice, I turned our conversation towards his handling of fame. After all, he had been selected for the West Indian Test team at the age of seventeen. Suddenly he had found himself thrust among his heroes as a figure for the back pages to devour.

Sir Gary tells me how he got down to scratch.

153

He replied: 'Fame can be taken in different lights and I like to think I have dealt with it in my own way, which I would have thought was a natural way. I think I realized that cricket was a game that was only going to be with me a certain time before leaving me and therefore I must not get carried away. I also played as a member of the team and not as an individual. That way I never got wrapped up in it the way some people do. I always remained the same with my old friends, having a drink with them, going to the same old places. As they say, you can walk with kings and you have to live with peasants.' He chuckled at his reworking of the line from Rudyard Kipling's 'If', which runs, 'If you can talk with crowds and keep your virtue, /Or walk with Kings – nor lose the common touch.'

He added: 'A lot is to do with your upbringing, and from being a little boy my parents had looked after me quite well so that when I got into the team at seventeen I had learned from those days that you respect people. I was really at an advantage because when I got into cricket I met some of my old friends. I met my great idol, Everton Weekes, and I just watched, listened, kept quiet and followed, and I think because of that I was able to get along with everybody and be respectful. It was easy to carry the fame at the beginning of my career without too much trouble.

'Now, just hold up against the wind'.

'I was a team man first. Everything I did was for the team. That is probably one of the reasons why I was so successful. On many occasions I went out there when the team needed me to do well and I put my head down and concentrated a lot harder. When the team was not in trouble it didn't really matter whether I made runs or not. Whenever I went in, the situation of the team was uppermost. If you ask anybody who has played with me they will certainly tell you I was a whole-hearted team man.'

Golf remained a mystery until he was twenty-five and then Sonny Ramadhin, the spin-bowling master of the post-war West Indian Calypso Cricketers, lured him onto a golf course near Canberra as the 1960 – 61 tour of Australia was drawing to a close. There was nostalgia in Sir Gary's eyes and voice as he recalled: 'Sonny was a good golfer with a very low single-figure handicap, two if I remember correctly. Every day he used to say to me: "Gary, how about playing some golf?" I used to tell him that golf looked too slow for me, that there was no excitement in just a hitting a little white ball, walking behind it and hitting it again. I used to quote the old saying, "You hit it, you find it and look a fool, you hit it again."

'After all this harassment from Sonny, four of us decided to give it a go on the golf course attached to the hotel. There was Wes Hall, Peter Lashley, Seymour Nurse and myself. Well, I have never felt so embarrassed. I put the ball down, a still ball, and went to hit it. I missed that ball by so much I could not believe it. Still, I started playing regularly and became very much in love with the game. The only setback was when I went to England to play county cricket with Nottinghamshire, thinking I would be able to get my game of golf every Sunday. Unfortunately, with the arrival of the Sunday League that was taken away from me so I didn't play much in my seven years there. As soon as I finished I went home and played almost every day. I think it's one of the greatest sports that I have ever played and I have tried quite a few of them.'

Sir Gary was always known for his sportsmanship and unfailing good humour, and he would clearly be at home with golf, a game renowned for its integrity, etiquette and honesty, which is run by people who are hard on those who cheat.

OPPOSITE A glimpse of Table Mountain as the clouds rise.

In recent years I have been sad to see batsmen wait for the umpire's finger before leaving the crease when they clearly know they have been caught by the wicket-keeper after nicking the ball. Have the old days really gone, I wondered.

'Let's put it this way,' Sir Gary said. 'There were some players who were "walkers" but they walked at convenient times. If they were on nought they would stand their ground. If they were on a hundred they would walk. They made it very difficult for umpires. There were other players who would always stand and wait for the umpire's decision regardless of whether they had nicked it because they felt it was the umpire's job to give them out and they had been victims of bad decisions in the past.

'I never subscribed to that view. I've always believed that if you nick the ball and are caught you should walk regardless of whether you are on nought, fifty or a hundred because the game should be played fairly and you know whether you have nicked it. If I nicked the ball and went on to make a hundred I would feel that I had cheated and would not be able to enjoy it. I was one of those who walked at all times. There were some situations, though, where you would get home town decisions. I've been through some of that in Pakistan. I was told by the players what was supposed to happen and it did. I was given out three times on the 1959 – 60 tour when I thought the ball would never have hit three more stumps and was told that it had been planned because I had made a lot of runs against Pakistan in the West Indies including my record score of 365 against them. English umpires who stand out in the middle, day in, day out, in county cricket and then Test cricket are the most competent.'

These days, Sir Gary works for the Barbados Tourism Board, playing his part, he says, in helping to promote the island's attractions. He is an elegant, personable man of the utmost integrity and, after touching on those bad umpiring decisions back in the sixties, I was anxious to know what he thought about such issues as ball-tampering, Ian Botham's place in cricket's history and why Sir Gary himself was not involved in some leading administrative role in West Indies cricket. He said, 'I only wanted to be a player. When I was made captain, as Sir Frank Worrell's choice, it took me some time to reply to his invitation because I had always lived with the players and I felt I would find it very difficult to turn around and tell them what to do. But the honour of captaining your country is such a great thing that after about two months of sitting on it I decided I had to accept. I never really wanted to go into administration because after I had finished playing I went to Australia to live for several years. It would have been very difficult to go back to the West Indies to take up a role as administrator when there were so many former players at home who knew more about the state of things than I did. In the West Indies there are so many experts you would be on a hiding to nothing.

'You ask me about ball tampering. I have heard a lot about it and doubted that anyone would carry anything in his pocket to scratch the ball. Then I heard that the Pakistan players used to carry bottle tops in their pockets to rough up one side of the ball to get it to swing more. I had never heard of it until about ten years ago, during the Pakistan era of Imran Khan and Sarfraz Nawaz and so on. To read about it really shocked me. One of the things that amazes me is that it all happened with the umpires standing there. Surely they should have been having a look. We used to use saliva or perspiration to rub in to keep one side of the ball shiny but actual ball tampering is something new to me. As for Ian Botham, he was a great player in his era. His bowling and his fielding were outstanding. Nobody could question that. He had the safest pair of hands and I liked his attacking spirit. He was the type of bowler you could depend on. He would throw everything at you. I thought his batting left something to be desired because when he went in he would throw the bat and it either came off or it didn't. People were always making excuses for him but great players make it happen. They go in, play themselves in and then get on top of the bowling and destroy it. He would throw the bat from ball one, and if things went his way he would make a lot of runs.'

We went on to talk a little about the new South Africa. Sir Gary's feelings towards Nelson Mandela, the president of South Africa, are: 'I look upon him as a tremendous person. After what Mr Mandela has been through and to come into politics and be the way he is, gentle and honest, takes a lot of doing after the punishment and imprisonment he was forced to endure. When I met him I thought he was a marvellous man.

157

We spent an hour together when he was on his way to a meeting. He knew a lot about his cricket, too. He said that Sir Donald Bradman had been his hero. Since then I have sent him photographs and pictures and I try to get in touch with him but he is such a busy man it is not easy. I simply applaud him.'

Sir Gary, too, has suffered from the effects of apartheid. Some years ago, at its height, he went to Rhodesia to play in a double wicket competition. I reminded him that because of this, in some areas of the media, he had been called a traitor. 'It was worse than that,' Sir Gary said. 'For about three months after I went back home I was front page, back page and middle page. I even had a priest come to my home to say prayers for me because he felt someone might kill me. Before I went to Rhodesia I asked a lot of questions and found that it was not the same as South Africa and that black footballers were playing for Rhodesia so they had mixtures. All the politicians in the West Indies knew for five weeks before I left that I had been invited, and if they felt that I should not go they had only to write to me. What happened was that when I was there I sat for a lunch period with the Rhodesian Prime Minister Ian Smith. I talked to him about certain things in Rhodesia and I will never forget his comment when he said: "There are a lot of people who live outside this country who do not know what is happening here and criticize me. I do not mind constructive criticism but people who know nothing about it should not really criticize." When I went back to the West Indies I made the mistake of saying I thought Ian Smith was a tremendous man and that was when it all happened. That was when the problems started and it was not easy. But going there was something I would do all over again if I had to because I didn't think I was breaking any laws and I was just going to play cricket.

'I don't have any hang-ups about the past. I certainly enjoyed coming to South Africa three or four years ago to try to help South Africa get back into first-class cricket and I think I was one of the people who was instrumental in doing so. I felt it was a job of mine to help them get back in because I thought so much of them.

'I had the opportunity of playing against South African teams when I was in Australia and I also captained teams containing some of the old South African players like Graeme Pollock, Eddie Barlow, Mike Procter and Barry Richards. It was a great pity when they were put out of first-class cricket. I was pleased when it all changed just as I am delighted to be in South Africa now.

'I know that South Africa will progress as years go by because it is a good sporting country. It may take a long time before there are four or five black players in the South African team and I hope the selectors will not do it just to prove to people that they are trying to have a mixed team. Very few of the young ones think about cricket. In the past they were always attracted to soccer.

'But there is progress here with the young black people and it is going so fast that I would not be surprised to see two or three of them in the South African team in the next fifteen years. Not so long ago a team came to Barbados from Transvaal, a mixed team of boys from the townships, whites, Indians and coloured boys. I had a look at them. Some were very good. The opportunity is there for them now and I am sure they will grasp it.'

159

The 18th green is narrow and he decides to lay up.

Any journey to South Africa would be incomplete without meeting Gary Player and it was to Sun City, a golfing and gambling oasis in the former homeland territory of Bophuthatswana, that we travelled. It was an interesting trip along remarkably good roads. I first visited Sun City fifteen years ago in the early days of the Million Dollar Challenge and decided that the place was a cross between Las Vegas and Disneyland, though not on the grand scale of either. The organizers had imported a cabaret of the Beach Boys and Lulu.

I met one of the Beach Boys – who were reasonable golfers – who told me that they were on with some British girl they had never heard of. I told him they had better be good because Lulu could easily steal the show. He gave me a knowing half-smile but when I saw him the next day, I heard that, sure enough, Lulu had taken the audience by storm.

Visits to Sun City always remind me of that trip but this time I was looking forward to seeing Gary at his second golfing creation in that part of the world, the Lost City Golf Club. Gary and I go back a long way, to 1954, and I have to confess that, along with John Jacobs and one or two

160

Gary Player
expounds his theory
of longevity.

others, I suggested to him, after his first few struggles on the European tour that perhaps he should return to South Africa and, if he was still interested in golf, find a job in a club shop as an assistant professional. If he looked after himself he might eventually get a full professional's job. Now, when I look at his glittering career, I begin to worry about some of my own judgements – but that was forty-two years ago. As we sat on the veranda outside the pro shop at Lost City, his views were as compelling as ever. He adores the course, which backs on to the Pilansberg game reserve. Apart from being a wonderful test of golf, it has some colourful and varied wild life. The grand attraction, though,

Gary Player, as bright as ever at 61.

is the crocodile pit to the left of the par-three, 13th green. If anyone were unlucky enough to fall in, they wouldn't come out alive, as a note on the scorecard makes plain. Gary believes that the course is a sterner challenge than the Country Club, where the Million Dollar Challenge was being held as we spoke and was won by Colin Montgomerie at the third extra hole in a play-off with local hero Ernie Els. He felt that the Challenge would not be transferred as the Country Club had become its traditional home.

Gary never ceases to amaze me. When we met this time he was moving towards his sixty-second birthday and he retains an immense enthusiasm for life. As I listened to him talk about his career I was interested to hear him use the word 'fortunate' frequently, and hesitated to say that he was 'proud' of anything. I wondered why, when he has won 150 tournaments around the world. He has 140 golf-course developments and has been an icon of the golfing world for many years.

Yet for all his self-effacement, he understands where he is in the world of golf and his plans for the future are still extensive. He would like to live to 120, and told me about the longevity of some people in Tibet. I can see him down on his stud farm at Colesberg in the Karoo with his mare Mistral Dancer, and the stallion that is the pride of his thoroughbred breeding and racing business, watching the yearlings progress. He also has plans to set up a golfing school there for young professionals.

OVERLEAF Is it Las Vegas or Disneyland – neither, it's Lost City.

As usual, no prompting was required after I probed him about some of the things he had said and done – his brushes with authority, suggestions that he used the rules to the limit, and those tales of 900 press-ups a day on his fingertips. How much was true and how much his own fantasy? He is one of only four people to have won all four of golf's majors – US Masters (three times), US Open, the Open Championship (three times) and the USPGA Championship (twice).

How did forty years of fame rest with him? He replied: 'Fame is nice but it's a fleeting glance, really. The Chinese have a great saying "Everything shall pass and it will all be gone." I am very grateful. I can't say I'm proud of what I have achieved in golf and sit back every week and say, "Gee, did I really win seven Australian Opens, thirteen South African Opens, all the major champions of the world, 159 tournaments?" I think the word is grateful. When I'm at the farm and I walk by my trophy cabinet and I see three British Opens and three US Masters, well, I'll tell you what I do. I never go to bed and miss one night ever, or during the day at some time, without saying thank you because it is a talent that is known only to you.

I had always felt that the Americans had been reluctant to give him proper recognition, I told him. He said, 'Americans in their own country are never going to say that anyone could beat them and that is understandable. They are never going to give me the recognition they gave Arnold Palmer and Jack Nicklaus. As for the exercises and push-ups, I do more today than I ever did when I was younger. It's a matter of circumstances when you're battling against those guys who fall out of bed with muscles and hit the ball a long way. You have to make up for it in another way. At lunchtime today I'll be in the gym squatting with three hundred pounds, doing thousands of sit-ups and getting these stomach muscles as strong, maybe stronger, than ever before. I want to show the world that I can win a tournament at seventy. The human being is made to live to a hundred and twenty. We are going to see that. We haven't scratched the surface of the human being's mind or body or his capabilities. The human being is an amazing animal.' Then I asked Gary what he thought about some major winners' loss of form – Ian Baker-Finch, Johnny Miller, Tom Watson, Seve Ballesteros. I thought he would have a forthright view and I was right.

He said: 'I've studied these four guys. Ian Baker-Finch has no idea of the knowledge of the swing. He thinks he does, but no. We were playing an exhibition and here was Ian, a man with a beautiful big turn and a lovely swing, and he said, "I've just had a lesson and I've had my swing changed." Tom Kite was with us and Ian asked us what we thought.

'I said, "Do you want me to be honest? You'll never win another golf tournament." It's a tragedy because he's a great human being who has just gone from bad to worse. Then you take Johnny Miller, a wonderful striker of the ball, who got the yips on the putting green and once that happens you can't be a great player any more. What happened to Tom Watson? He was America's last superstar. He hits the ball better now than he did in his prime but he got the yips and when that happens you stop winning. Whether it's all in the mind is a debatable issue. Everybody has tried to work out why people get the yips. Then there is Seve. He's confused about the golf swing. He's trying all sorts of things. We all did that a little bit but we still had certain movements that were at the heart of the golf swing. Those guys have lost the theoretical side. I watch them play and they don't understand the theory.

'There are all these great gurus they talk about. They go to pros who cannot break eighty and have them telling them how to play. It's not possible. A man who can't break eighty can't tell you how to play golf when the flag is in the back right hand corner and you need a four for a million dollars. He can tell you what he thinks and what he has experimented but he has never been in that situation in his life. I want to go to Lee Trevino when I have a lesson because there is a man who is street smart. He knows what is needed. He knows the theory of the game.' The conversation raced on and I could not help thinking of the contrasts that surround Gary.

He has his farm on the Karoo, a beautiful home, Blair Atholl, an hour or so north of Johannesburg, where more horses are stabled, and he runs a school for four hundred black children in the grounds. The primitive bus does a two-hundred-and-fifty-mile round trip journey every day collecting and delivering the children from their homes. But the other side of South Africa, the breakdown of law and order, the escalating incidence of street crime, has made downtown Johannesburg almost a no-go area.

165

The politicians we met later, Andrew Mlangeni and F. W. de Klerk, had their own profound views on that and so did Gary: 'It is frightening and it is demoralizing. I had dinner with US President Eisenhower once and he said, "Gary, a country has to have security. I am a great believer in freedom but once you go over the brink of freedom into lack of discipline you are in trouble. People will not spend. They will not invest and your economy will tumble." Unless we are careful that is what is going to happen in South Africa but we have a better, far more capable government with our black people than we had with our white. Across the board they are more brilliant. They are great people who spent time in exile and had terrible things occur to them and their families. That is why they should come in now, having had that experience, to curb and stop the violence right away.

166

'South Africa has a great future because we have great people but if we do not curb our violence we will not survive. There are great portfolios in the world that do not have South Africa on their books for investment right now. I have been through all the changes and seen it all.

'I am pleased that I have lived to see this great change in South Africa. I believe in affirmative action because we denied the black the opportunity. If a white went for a job with a black, the white automatically got it. That is why I had my school during the apartheid era and not after it. It has given me great joy. The mothers can leave the children and know they are safe.'

Gary was preparing to set off for another season on the US Seniors Tour, there were golf course developments to inspect, money to be raised for the Gary Player Foundation (his school) and so on. When will it all come to an end?

'I don't want to go into the tournament circuit and be shooting seventy-eights and seventy-nines like I see some champions doing. I can still play well. The fact that I had six second places in 1996 showed that I was only that much from six firsts. My exemption from the British Open Championship, which is the best in the world, runs out in 2000 when, God willing, I will have played forty-six straight Opens. Then I will retire but if they wanted to give me an extra one as a present the way they did with Arnold I would accept it and that would be it after 2001. I will see how I am playing on the Senior Tour but they have a

Well, we've known each other a long time!

167

Super Seniors now. Do you know that in 1974 I won the US Masters, the British Open and six other tournaments and made $177,000? On the Super Seniors for players aged sixty and over I made $145,000, winning three. Money is no criterion any more. People should stop talking about money and judge players on what events they win. Only your wife and your dog knows who finishes second.

'I am very blessed, very fortunate and that is why the first word I used when we met was "grateful". I love my country. I love the people in my country. I love the challenge of golf.

'We have been fortunate. We would travel across the country to play in a pro-am for a hundred dollars. Now you have a million-dollar first prize and a guy says, "Well, it's a bit far and the wife says I've been away from home too much." If it was me, pal, I'd get in a boat and row over.

'Tiger Woods starts with a sixty-million-dollar contract. It's beyond all of our imaginations. Isn't he lucky? He's half black, he's half Asian. All of Asia is pulling for him like crazy, all the blacks in the world are pulling for him. In fact all the whites and everybody else is pulling for him. This is so exciting. He has, in my opinion, the greatest fundamentals of the golf swing of all the young players I have seen in the world.'

The old pro was talking about a fearless youngster entering the precarious world of tournament golf that few have mastered with greater authority than Gary Player, whose tenacity and determination were worn like a badge. There had been incidents, though, that had irked some people. I recalled a tense moment at the thirty-seventh hole in the 1968 World Matchplay Championship semi-final at Wentworth. Gary, who was playing Tony Jacklin, was about to make a putt when he heard a voice in the crowd saying, "Miss it, miss it." He holed the ball and walked straight across to give the spectator a finger-wagging rebuke. Jacklin stood back, waiting for the row to subside, then missed the putt he needed to stay in the match. He reacted as though Gary had purposely distracted him and the crowd were equally unimpressed.

'Don't you think golfers are prone to making responses?' Gary asked. 'Aren't we all? I had to putt with that guy shouting and I holed it. Tony misses and people make excuses for him. We all have to face criticisms. Arnold Palmer had some terrible things written about him. I once saw Jack Nicklaus throw down *Sports Illustrated* because he was so upset at what they had written about him. People used to boo when he made a birdie and cheer when he made a bogey. He overcame unbelievable things.

'As far as the rules were concerned, I always asked for the official to give a ruling. I remember once leading a tournament in Memphis when my ball came to rest in ground under repair. The rules man told me where to drop but Hubert Green disputed it. I said, "Hubert, I've got you by two shots. I'm going to beat you anyway. If you want me to drop it in a divot I'll do that." The official was not amused and said if I did not drop it as he had said I would be penalized two shots. End of story. I can say, fortunately, I am happy that I can go to my grave without any worries.'

The clubhouse at Lost City is an extravagant creation with a façade seemingly composed of giant rocks that you suspect had been hewn from some distant hillside and hauled slowly at great expense to the site. It was a disappointment to learn that it is made of plaster applied to a framework and painted. It was very cleverly done, though.

Here I was to have a knock with Andrew Mlangeni – and, for once, I was tempted to forget golf and talk about politics but Mr Mlangeni's enthusiasm for the game turned out to be as rich as his love of Africa. He showed no bitterness at having spent fifteen years in a tiny cell on Robben Island but I wondered what he was thinking as he surveyed the outrageous opulence of the rich man's playground at the Sun Palace.

For a man of seventy-one his golf swing was remarkably fluid. All those hours swinging a pick axe in the quarry on Robben Island had clearly given him wrists of steel. He knew little of who I was in a golfing sense and when we came to the crocodile hole with its elevated tee and the green 160 yards away he told me I would need more than the 6-iron I had in my hand. He liked the challenge of the hole and impressively hit three balls onto the green, using his 4-iron.

I rattled one among the crocodiles, which may have resulted in one of them having indigestion later, but when my next, with the 6-iron, went to the back of the green, I think he began to realise that I might have played the game before. Eventually, though, I felt I could not wait to get back to the clubhouse to talk to Mr Mlangeni about golf and politics. How does a black man, brought up in the poverty of the townships, get involved in a game of colonial élitism?

OVERLEAF The clubhouse at Lost City where I met Gary Player.

169

Andrew Mlangeni
– 26 years in
prison because of
his beliefs.

He said: 'I was born on the sixth of June 1925, and I first became involved in golf in 1937 when I was a caddie. I was only a kiddie but I started to play seriously in 1947 after I had left school and then I played until 1953. We just used to play on any piece of barren ground. We made our own course with sand "greens". I played on a proper course only after I came out of prison. Such things were unknown to Africans at the time.'

At risk of appearing flippant I suggested that had he stayed in golf instead of moving into politics in 1945 he might have become the Tiger Woods of his day. He told me, very quietly: 'I became interested in politics with the hope that I might be able to make a contribution to changing the conditions of our people. One, the pass system where people were being raided almost on a daily basis and if you did not have your pass, an identity card, you were jailed. Two, there were the raids on the townships on our mothers and sisters who were brewing African beer in order to make a living. Those two things were uppermost in my mind. I saw how my people suffered and I decided to join the organization which was already fighting the evil system.'

He linked up with the ANC. As a young man he had been to China. I asked him why. He laughed aloud as he said: 'It is an open secret that I was one of the first people to be sent out of the country for military training. When the ANC was banned in 1960 we had no alternative but to take up arms because the Nationalist Party government was already saying that if any other organization was formed with similar aims as the ANC it would be banned in twenty-four hours. I saw no alternative but to go underground and operate from there.

'I remember in 1958, Helen Suzman of the liberal Progressive Party, being a lone voice when she told the Government that they would be making a very serious mistake if they banned the ANC because the organization would then go underground and no one would know what we were up to.

'The arrest was a different story. Nelson Mandela was already operating secretly, working towards forming the MK, the military wing of the ANC. When I came back from my training in China I discovered that Nelson had already been arrested and four years after my return I was snapped up too. Robben Island was divided into a number of sections. We were the so-called leaders, about thirty of us from various political organizations such as ANC, PAC [Pan Africanist Congress], the Unity

OVERLEAF Some of the waters at the Lost City golf course.

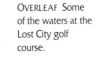

Andrew Mlangeni has wrists like steel from all the quarry work.

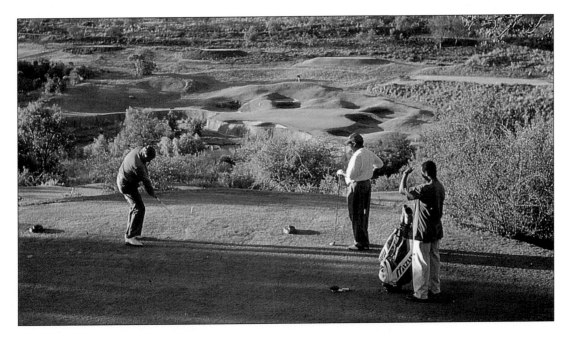

Movement, SWAPO [South-West Africa People's Organisation] and so on. The greater part of the prison population was in other sections. We lived in single cells, nine feet by seven feet. Prison opened at seven in the morning and after washing and breakfast, we were taken to work in the quarry. We worked at the lime quarry for more than fifteen years, digging and shovelling with no purpose at all.

'The other people in the prison, about a thousand of them, did completely different kinds of work. Most of the people who worked at the quarry now wear spectacles because the constant glare of the sun on the lime was damaging. Mandela suffered in this way. We used to meet while we were working. We were studying at the quarry, teaching other people while we were digging. We used the ground to write figures or letters to teach some of those who had never been to school. Some of them today are ministers. I am not going to mention names but one fellow who could hardly write his name is now a minister in Natal. Of course, being there was a punishment but it was useful in that we built that prison for ourselves. There were only a few loose structures when we arrived.

'After the student uprising in Soweto in 1976 a new crop of prisoners arrived. They were lawyers and young men with degrees and they took over from us, so to speak, and were sent to the lime quarries. We were taken along to the shore to pull out seaweed that was dragged out to dry. Once dried we loaded it onto lorries. It was taken to a small factory that turned it into a powder. It was then sent to Japan and used for many things. We managed to get the word out that South Africa was using prison labour to produce and export things to other countries and Japan was threatened by many countries. The prison authorities stopped all this. They had no work for us. It was the digging and shovelling that kept me going.'

The ANC, now in power in South Africa, is looking forward with Mr Mlangeni to bringing about change. Mr Mlangeni did not shy away from discussing the problems of the new South Africa as the standard bearer of liberation, racial equality and fair government.

Weighing his words carefully, he said: 'We say right from the beginning, "Chaps, you have imprisoned us, you have sent people into exile, you have killed our children but, for the sake of the country, we are prepared to work together with you. Let's forgive the past, though we cannot forget it. Let everyone work together and live happily together." That is the philosophy of the ANC. It must work but we cannot stop those who want to go their own way. We are saying that South Africa belongs to *all* the people. Our economy is in tatters, let us build it together. Let us try to improve the living conditions of everybody, blacks and whites. Don't run away to Britain, Australia, Canada and the United States. Stay and help this country.

'The movement is going forward. We have destroyed the barriers that prevented people from doing certain things and entering certain universities and doing certain types of work. All that has happened since 1994 and we are still going through the discriminatory laws. We have inherited a bankrupt state. That is why our president has been around the world thanking countries for their support when we were fighting apartheid but now asking them to re-invest so that we can create jobs.

'We want everybody to have a better life. People want to work in order to make a living. Investments are not coming in fast enough to create jobs. That is why there is still violence in the country. It is not political violence but what is left is stealing. The level of theft is horrendous. It had reached proportions that are unacceptable to us and to the Government. Still I am looking forward to the future with great hope. We may not have fulfilled all our promises but we are building houses, improving schooling and medical assistance and so on.'

I could not let him go without canvassing his views on F. W. de Klerk, currently leader of the opposition, the National Party, who helped to knock down the walls of apartheid and served during the transition as the country's vice-president alongside Mandela. He has been president himself during years of riots, upheavals and border skirmishes when most of the rest of the world had condemned South Africa to isolation.

A back-handed compliment was returned: 'Mr de Klerk became realistic when we were in

177

F.W. de Klerk, one of the dismantlers of apartheid.

prison. He realized that South Africa was losing too much in fighting wars beyond our borders. He knew that ultimately he would have to sit around the table and discuss with his enemies – the black people of the ANC.

'When he took over as president from P. W. Botha he immediately said: "Let us accede to the ANC demand that we sit and discuss." In that sense he made a contribution to the change. He made a contribution also in the drafting of the new constitution of South Africa. In that sense he and his party were helpful. Some of his men became unpopular in the process because the hard-liners thought they were giving too much to the ANC. We had to have compromises and without them we would not be where we are today. It is a great pity that they have withdrawn from the Government of National Unity. We are sorry about that. They have said what is the point of going to bed with a woman who does not love you, inferring that they have been in bed with the ANC but realized they would be rejected in the 1999 elections anyway. There is no way the National Party can ever win

Crossing the water at Silver Lakes with F.W. de Klerk.

Golf, the great escape for any politician.

the elections again and they know it. That is why they wanted the Government of National Unity to continue after 1999 to make certain that the whites, Afrikaners in particular, have a say in running the country. We prefer a multi-party democracy. We do not like coalitions. Win some votes, get into Parliament. You can criticize the ANC if you like. We accept that.'

It had not been my intention to turn this South African odyssey into a political debate but it is impossible to move around this vast and interesting country without being embroiled in arguments concerning the past and the future. Now we were to meet Mr de Klerk in the clubhouse of Silver Lakes Golf Club, on the edge of Pretoria, to the north of Johannesburg and a couple of hours' drive from Sun City. On the stroke of nine, the appointed hour, he walked in with a security man who doubled as his caddie.

Almost, but not quite. F.W. de Klerk on the 9th at Silver Lakes.

I was immediately struck by Mr de Klerk's look of casual elegance. the Dunhill blazer, dark grey trousers, and an expensive pair of moccasin-type shoes. He had always appeared as a flinty-eyed hard man in his photographs, but on this sunny Monday morning he was benign. He sat down, immediately reached for a cigarette and smoked profusely throughout the morning. He told me that he was not proud that he regularly got through thirty or forty a day. He appeared slightly hesitant, even nervous, about the interview and, like all politicians, he wanted to know my line of questioning in advance so that he would not be taken unawares.

I told him that I just wanted to talk about golf and the way things have changed in South Africa. We could not play a full round because later that day at Silver Lakes he was taking part in a pro-am for the benefit of one of his favourite charities, the Women's Outreach Foundation, for which his wife, Marike, works tirelessly. Its aim is to help women in rural areas and the organization hopes to bolster its funds with industrial companies sponsoring holes at Silver Lakes. I bumped into some old friends on the practice ground: John Bland, who spent many years on the European tour and is now making a fortune on the US Seniors tour, was there along with Dennis Hutchinson, another great character who has spent a lot of time in Europe.

Mr de Klerk and I went out to the ninth hole to have a look at his swing. He was relaxed and determined to enjoy his day with no mention of politics on the golf course. The hole is quite a teaser, 190 yards from the back tees across a big lake. We were a few yards further forward. A 7-wood for him and a 6-iron for me.

He had a couple of 'mulligans' after the water had devoured a couple of balls but then the shot that counted landed in a right-hand bunker while I was at the back of the green, with, as they say, a lot of golf left in it. He got out and two putted for a four (nett three) as I contemplated a nightmare putt of 60 feet with a 5-foot borrow. I did not strike it particularly well, hitting the ball above the equator on the bottom of the blade. It ran towards the top of the slope, toppled over the crest and went towards the hole. As soon as I saw my caddie doing a subdued war dance I realized it was going to be close and, sure enough, it fell in. A win for me – a monster putt holed by accident.

Before we sat down for the interview on the lawn by the lake Mr de Klerk was concerned as to where he would be placed. Apparently he had been interviewed by someone who had given him a tough time while facing the sun, which had made him appear hard. I wondered why, as a seasoned politician, he had allowed this to happen. He gave the impression of being good at politics and the law, and managed to convey his

181

At Silver Lakes, where F.W. de Klerk was impressed by my monster putt.

Fantasy land – the
Palace at Lost City.

183

efforts towards the betterment of people in South Africa in an undemonstrative way. He spoke eloquently and it came as no surprise to find him expecting to see the return of his party in the 1999 elections.

What wrong-footed me a little was that he had not heard of Andrew Mlangeni, and yet the two are supposed to be working towards the common aim – albeit on opposite sides of the political fence – of making South Africa the great country they believe it can be. But De Klerk was relatively complimentary about the ANC's two years in office.

His golf, he said, was a passion he had retained since his youth. Everybody had told him it was good for business but after just three games he realized it was good for him and, as he said: 'I then started playing for the sheer pleasure of it. I reached a handicap of 20. Then we had a family and I found the game took me away from my wife and kids too much. I stopped playing and only started again when I was getting lonely at weekends when my kids were leaving me at home alone around the age of forty-six.'

I wanted to ask him about the South African situation because crime is a problem. Perhaps the move to change the nation had accelerated too quickly? Could South Africa deliver anything so fast? De Klerk did not hide behind parliamentary gobbledegook when he replied: 'It can be done. It will require wise political leadership. We have a problem of frustrated expectations because some wild promises were made. One needs to go to the people to explain that it will take time. We can achieve progress in a year but some things may take ten or even fifteen. We need to build confidence among investors. Jobs top the list of what people want.

'When my party received the mandate from the white electorate, which said we have finished with apartheid, there would be one South Africa with one citizenship and one vote without any form of racial discrimination, many people were shocked. But I had broad support except for smaller parties which split away from us to the right. They called me a traitor and still do. I am no longer a white leader representing white interests in South Africa. I am a leader of a moderate party of the centre, which is representative of white and black, coloured and Indian, and throughout the structures of our National Party you will find in leadership positions people from all our population groups.

'The ANC has a problem. The cement that kept them together was to overthrow the old regime, as they called us, to win the fight against apartheid. That brought together under one umbrella communists and non-communists, hard-line socialists and pragmatists. Now that goal has disappeared, the cement no longer exists. The ANC is really an organization still in transition and in need of finding and redefining itself. Somehow in South Africa there will come about a fundamental political realignment. I am trying to play a role to ensure that it will be according to proven values across the world that will unite the majority of all decent, hard-working, good and religious South Africans into a broad political movement, which will say to the radicalists on the left and the right, that they will not ruin this wonderful country because South Africa has the potential to become a real world player.'

185

Travelling around by road had given me some insight into the poverty of the squatter camps and townships. Reports of violent crime and theft filled the newspapers. How did Mr de Klerk feel about poverty, crime and the future?

'Poverty is not the result of lack of effort,' he said. 'An inherent part of our problem is our high birth-rate. The school population grows by more than four per cent every year. We have an inheritance from an underdeveloped population that continues to grow too fast and which must be brought along the route of modernization. Smaller families, concentration on standards and upgrading our facilities – we have plans for that.

'I can still truthfully say that I believe it is going to be a good place and I don't think one should take a short-term view about management mistakes that are being made. Trust the new democratic system to take care of that as years go by. There is a broad underlying consensus of what needs to be done. I have confidence in the future although I am critical in the short term about a number of important aspects.

'In the two crucial years during which we served in the Government of National Unity, we and the ANC succeeded in agreeing on an anti-crime strategy. Some aspects of it have been implemented and the latest figures show a reasonable improvement in some areas where some crimes were unacceptably high. I am confident that we can come to grips with crime. But there is a longer-term problem and it has two sides to it. One is economic deprivation. If we can resolve the economic situation it will have a

Take me to the Sabi
Sabi big game.

186

marked effect on crime. The other one is more difficult. In the years of
revolutionary onslaught people were taught to break the law. So we sit
with a heritage of not to play to the rules. That is an attitudinal problem
that we will have to change in the hearts and minds of young South
Africans and children. That is a challenge we need to accept.'

De Klerk's firm handshake as he left us for the first tee was that of a
man optimistic about this great country's future. Everything he and
Mlangeni had said rang with the hope that South Africa, a compelling
land of contrasts and smiles and richness, was about to unite in a way
that would write one of the most wonderful stories of the century.

They all toast the 'new' South Africa and our journey helped us to
understand why. There is the glory of the Cape, the majesty of the
mountains, the vastness of the veldt, the animals of the bush and so
much more under what is, truly, a Big Sky. Being there, seeing the
bright eyes at Gary Player's school and youngsters elsewhere proud and
striving in their neat uniforms as they walk mile upon mile to school,

only enhances the visitor's feelings of well-being; that something good is happening in a land where trouble used to be a constant brew.

We had come a long way from the drenching in Scotland, through the Arizona desert, to the timelessness of Spain, the cascading surf of Hawaii to this, journey's end, in the world's new land of opportunity. It would be a joy to go round again, in another direction.

187

Index

ACKNOWLEDGEMENTS

Peter Alliss wishes to thank the following
generous supporters of his travels:
Rover Group Ltd.,
Mizuno Corporation, Cross Creek International,
Titleist and Footjoy, Alfred Dunhill, Powakaddy.
Thanks are also due to the following in the individual countries -
Scotland:Rover Group, Loch Lomond Golf Club, Dunbartonshire
Enterprise, Carnegie Club at Skibo Castle, Highlands of Scotland
Tourist Board, Royal Dornoch Golf Club, Golf Scotland, Cameron
House Hotel, Links Hotel; Arizona/New Mexico: Land Rover
North America Inc., Arizona Office of Tourism, Desert Mountain
Properties, Las Campanas, Scottsdale Chamber of Commerce,
Sedona Golf Club, Scottsdale Princess Resort; Hawaii: Land Rover
North America Inc., Hawaii Visitors and Convention Bureau,
Turtle Bay Hilton, The Links at Kuilima, Aloha Airlines, Creative
Leisure International, The Lanai Company, Manele Bay Hotel,
The Experience at Koele, Kapalua Villas, Kapalua Golf Course,
Kapalua Resort; South Africa: Land Rover South Africa, SAA—
South African Airways, Steenberg Country Hotel and Golf Club,
Palace at Lost City, Sun International, Sun City Hotel, Silver
Lakes Golf Club, Sabi Sabi Game Reserve; Spain: Rover Group
Spain, Gibraltar Airways, Valderrama Golf Club, La Cañada Golf
Club, Rio Tinto Zinc Golf Club; Thailand: Thai Airways
International, Tourism Authority of Thailand, Planet Golf, Blue
Canyon Country Club, Chiva Som International Health Resort,
Nichigo Resort and Country Club.

Thank you, too, to those excellent photographers who have provided the illustrations in this book: Brian Morgan, Phil Sheldon,
Alexander Franklin, Scott D. Christopher and Richard Maack.

VIDEO

The companion video, 'A Golfer's Travels with Peter Alliss' is available now at £10.99 from Clear Vision Video on 0181-292-4875, PO Box 148, Enfield, Middlesex or from all good video stores. The 60-minute tape features exclusive commentary by Peter Alliss as he advises and analyses his guests' performances over some of the most spectacular signature holes in the world.

TRAVEL CLUB

You may want to travel and play in the footsteps of Peter Alliss and his guests. Gullivers Sports Travel will customise a travel package for you and your family or friends to one or more of the locations. Further information is available from Gullivers on 01684-299099, or write to: Peter Alliss's Footsteps, Fiddington Manor, Tewkesbury, Gloucestershire GL20 7BJ.